Shoot! ANNUAL 1987

S0-CFG-518

3. Aberdeen won their first European trophy when they beat a famous Spanish side 2-1 in Gothenburg in 1983.
a) Which competition did Aberdeen win and who were their opponents?
b) Is John Hewitt, Eric Black or Mark McGhee pictured heading home the winning goal?
c) Which Scottish international skippered Aberdeen on the night and partners Alex McLeish in the heart of their defence?
d) One other British club has won this European trophy during the Eighties. Can you name the team and the year?

4. Aston Villa became the third English club to win the European Cup in the space of six years after their 1-0 win over Bayern Munich in 1982.
a) The picture shows Gary Shaw, Tony Morley and Peter Withe holding the trophy. Which one of the three cracked home the winning goal?
b) Bayern Munich play in the French, German or Spanish League?
c) Villa made a unique substitution in the Final. After only ten minutes young goalkeeper Nigel Spink replaced which international?

SBN 85037-906-7

£3.25

PAUL DAVIS GRABS GUNNERS GLORY

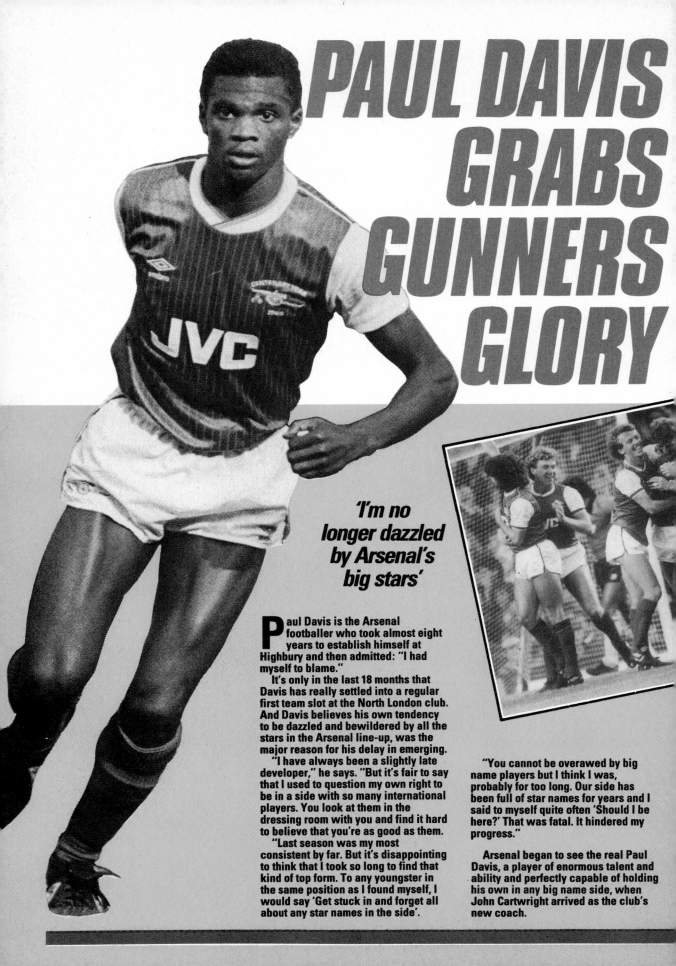

'I'm no longer dazzled by Arsenal's big stars'

Paul Davis is the Arsenal footballer who took almost eight years to establish himself at Highbury and then admitted: "I had myself to blame."

It's only in the last 18 months that Davis has really settled into a regular first team slot at the North London club. And Davis believes his own tendency to be dazzled and bewildered by all the stars in the Arsenal line-up, was the major reason for his delay in emerging.

"I have always been a slightly late developer," he says. "But it's fair to say that I used to question my own right to be in a side with so many international players. You look at them in the dressing room with you and find it hard to believe that you're as good as them.

"Last season was my most consistent by far. But it's disappointing to think that I took so long to find that kind of top form. To any youngster in the same position as I found myself, I would say 'Get stuck in and forget all about any star names in the side'.

"You cannot be overawed by big name players but I think I was, probably for too long. Our side has been full of star names for years and I said to myself quite often 'Should I be here?' That was fatal. It hindered my progress."

Arsenal began to see the real Paul Davis, a player of enormous talent and ability and perfectly capable of holding his own in any big name side, when John Cartwright arrived as the club's new coach.

Paul cracks the winning goal against Manchester City at Highbury. It's this form that has established him as a regular at Arsenal.

Paul lacked confidence before John Cartwright (right) arrived.

regarded as a superbly talented player with a big future.

But many years since have produced only frustration. Indeed, Davis now admits the thought of leaving Arsenal went through his mind on more than one occasion.

"It has probably taken me longer than it should have done to succeed here. And during some of those frustrating years, I began to wonder if I would ever make it at Arsenal. You begin to wonder whether you are good enough to be successful at such a big club as Arsenal.

Struggling

"But I stuck it out and it has come right for me. And I'm glad I did. Because I believe in the next few years, I can show the First Division what I'm really capable of. In the days when I was struggling, people would say 'Don't worry about the internationals'.

"But that is easier said than done. I admit I was a bit star struck at certain times."

Many youngsters like Paul have come through the Highbury talent factory in the past year or so to prove that First Division clubs don't always have to spend fortunes on recruiting players of talent.

Davis adds: "Since this last season, I have felt far more comfortable in the side. I'm also more positive in all I do as well as my attitude. I'm pleased with the way things have gone for me recently and I believe Highbury fans will see the real me in the future."

"I had a great relationship with John — he got me thinking in a far more positive manner. I have more belief and self confidence and nowadays, I don't doubt my ability to go out there and do well. For years I was lacking that.

"But John made me confident simply by talking to me. He talks about the team game but also your own individual contribution. He was a big help to me and all the other young lads, too.

Naturally it came as a shock when

he and Don Howe left."

Arsenal needed Davis to assert his authority far more than he had been doing. "It's all about taking control of the situation, rather than waiting for things to happen" he says.

"I'm still not as dominating as I would like to be but I'm trying to take command far more than I used to. That comes down to having complete faith in your ability."

Davis joined Arsenal straight from school at 16 and made his first team debut two years later. Early on, he was

The new LIVER

Kenny Dalglish gave Liverpool a severe reminder of their past when he succeeded Joe Fagan as manager at Anfield in May, 1985.

The brilliant Scot, who became the youngest manager in the First Division — and the only player-boss at that level, 'did a Bill Shankly'.

Shankly took the reins at Anfield in December, 1959 and within weeks had drawn up a list of 24 players he

Steve McMahon (left) settled into the Liverpool midfield as soon as he arrived from Aston Villa. (Above) Steve Nicol was a natural replacement for Phil Neal at right-back.

POOL

wanted to sell. Within 12 months they were gone. Liverpool developed into the best team in Europe.

Dalglish was equally tough. He sold Alan Kennedy to Sunderland, Phil Thompson to Sheffield United, made it clear Phil Neal was on the way out of his plans — and built for the future.

Players such as Craig Johnston and Jan Molby, disillusioned under Fagan, changed their minds and stayed for manager Kenny Dalglish.

As the Liverpool squad changed and became younger, so Dalglish let his own playing days wind down to the bench and, finally, emergency appearances only.

Steve McMahon was signed from Aston Villa and quickly became a success with the fans.

A former Everton player and a local lad, McMahon was desperate to return to Merseyside and repaid his new manager with goals, flair and sheer hard work in a new-look midfield.

With Neal on the way out, Steve Nicol, a hard-tackling and skilful young Scotland cap was moved from a midfield to right-back — and became a quality defender.

Nicol's ability to overlap, see openings for the forwards, cover and tackle made him a perfect replacement for the former England stalwart Neal.

Jim Beglin's consistent form left Dalglish with no alternative but to allow Kennedy to leave.

Beglin, a gifted Irishman and already playing for the Republic, was described by Wales striker Ian Rush as: "The most exciting and most talented young player at Anfield."

He has settled down well at left-back, sweeping into the attack, swinging over superb crosses and pushing up on opponents, driving them into their own half.

Bruce Grobbelaar held his place as number one goalkeeper, forcing Bob

CONTINUED

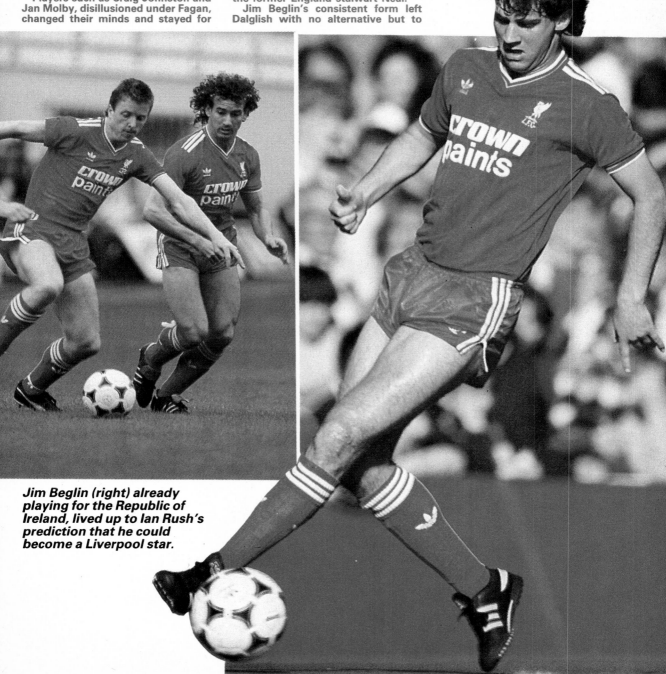

Jim Beglin (right) already playing for the Republic of Ireland, lived up to Ian Rush's prediction that he could become a Liverpool star.

CONTINUED

Bolder to seek a new club. He began being transferred to Sunderland knowing his first team chances at Anfield were limited.

That left Dalglish seeking a new understudy. He opted for Mike Hooper from Wrexham.

The tall youngster, nicknamed 'Hoops' arrived without a driving licence but armed with a University degree.

What mattered was the speed at which he settled into Liverpool's ways and became a part of the set-up.

Said Rush: "He is just the right kind of personality for the joking and pranks that go on in our dressing room."

But the signing that caught all of football off guard was Wayne Harrison, a 17 year old striker who was just

Kenny Dalglish meets new 'keeper Mike Hooper at Anfield. Wayne Harrison, playing in Liverpool strip for the first time during a reserve match.

beginning to make a name at Oldham.

While other managers started to watch him and discuss him, Joe Fagan, the man who was to give way to Kenny Dalglish, swooped.

Harrison was signed in a blaze of publicity ... then loaned back to Oldham for the rest of season 1984-85.

"I want the lad to feel settled and relaxed," said Dalglish: "So I had a chat with Oldham manager Joe Royle.

"Wayne went back to his club and, after the initial fuss, got on with learn-

ing his trade. That way I was assured the lad continued playing League football, improved and developed."

Harrison arrived at Anfield at the start of the next season and, as Rush explained: "Stood out as a natural striker.

"He has pace, a quick brain and lovely skills on the ball. I predict a big future for him if he continues to develop the way he is going."

Another of the young players who comprise the 'new' Liverpool.

CLOSE ENCOUNTER as Aston Villa's midfield star Steve Hodge and Colin Walsh of Nottingham Forest do battle in last season's match at Villa Park.

Through getting injured so much, do you think you let down Manchester United? Couldn't you be more careful?

Robson: If I'm on the sidelines that is no use at all to my manager. I don't go out of my way to get injured but when you become as involved as I do in midfield tackling, you suffer these knocks. I can't change my style, I go in hard, always have done, and sometimes finish up getting the worst of it.

What do you enjoy most, captaining England or Manchester United?

Robson: They're very different jobs. Nothing has been more important to my career than being asked to captain England. England manager Bobby Robson made me realise the honour involved in that job. He, and Ron Greenwood, restored pride to England after a few years when our international players had lost their way. I'd play for England for nothing! To be captain of Manchester United is the greatest reward in League football.

Your goal-scoring is erratic, one month scoring with every shot, the next a barren spell. Can you explain that?

Robson: I know what you mean. At Manchester United I try to average 15 goals a season from midfield — and my England record is not bad. I tend to go scoreless when the manager has asked me to play a more defensive midfield role. There have been days I can well remember when I was happy to sit back at Old Trafford with Norman Whiteside, Jesper Olsen, Gordon Strachan, Mark Hughes, Frank Stapleton and Peter Barnes bursting forward for a crack at goal. If you've got too many men up front you tend to leak goals at the back. England has been the same. If the line-up allows, I'll go forward and, hopefully, score goals.

Isn't it true that Manchester United never properly replaced Ray Wilkins?

Robson: I can't accept that as well as Ray played for Manchester United. Give Gordon Strachan credit for what his arrival did for Old Trafford. We changed our style when Ray left. In many respects I think it was better.

You're always going on about Norman Whiteside. What's so special about him?

Robson: That sounds a rather sour question. Norman's record says more than anything I can tell you. He was the youngest player to appear in a World Cup Finals, in 1982, and won F.A. Cup medals all before the age of 20. My bet is that Norman will be around the Irish scene long enough to threaten Pat Jennings' record number of caps for

MAKE ENGLAND

Norman Whiteside in determined mood against another of football's fiery fighters ... Gary Waddock of QPR.

that country. Norman reminds me so much of the former Liverpool and England man, Ray Kennedy. Big, strong, surprising control, loves to score goals and is a formidable opponent.

Ian Rush has said that Mark Hughes, the Welsh and Manchester United striker, is a scorer of goals but not a great goalscorer? Do you agree?

Robson: I know what Ian means. When he talks about 'great goalscorers', Ian is referring to that special breed of target-man who can score with screamers from 30 yards — or tuck them in the net from two feet. Jimmy Greaves, Denis Law and Rush himself are part of that elite. Kerry Dixon is another who will

ME SWEEPER

poke the ball home with his knee if that is the only way to score a goal. Mark Hughes does a lot of his work from deeper positions — but he's world class in a different way from Jimmy, Denis and company.

How much longer will you play for England?

Robson: Until I drop dead! They'll have to carry me into exile on some remote island in the South Pacific to keep me away from the England camp. More seriously, two, three, maybe the 1990 World Cup. I'll be 33 that year and will have to be in exceptional form to remain in the team that long. I'll only get a game if I'm worth my place. It's been suggested I could play at sweeper in the Franz Beckenbauer role of his later years in the West German team. England have never really played with a sweeper but maybe I can convince Bobby Robson he needs one!

CONTINUED OVERLEAF

The exciting skills of Gordon Strachan (right) have helped United fans forget Ray Wilkins.

CONTINUED

Why are wingers like John Barnes, Chris Waddle and Peter Barnes so erratic?

Robson: Maybe because we don't give them enough of the ball. How can you play if you're standing on the wing starved of service? Great wingers like Tom Finney and Stan Matthews complained in their day about lack of service. Their style also means that they will lose the ball occasionally. If you try to waltz round a full-back who is playing out of his skin, you can find yourself robbed. Your team-mates moan like hell, the boss hides his head in his hands, and the crowd give you the bird. I've told John and Chris at England level, and Peter at Old Trafford, that consistency is the name of the game. But I'd rather have 20 minutes of John Barnes' magic than 90 minutes of uninspired slog by some of these people who think they are wingers but aren't. You've forgotten to mention Pat

Nevin. I don't know whether he's erratic, but he's certainly magic. Wingers are wonderful, I reckon.

Who are the greatest players you've seen at home and abroad?

Robson: I shall never tire of playing against Michel Platini, the Napoleon of the French midfield. Wonderful artistry — and he scores goals. Paolo Rossi, on song, was sensational for Italy in the 1982 World Cup. Maradona's magic speaks for itself but he'd get a piece of my mind about behaving himself if I was his captain. He's too much 'John McEnroe' for my liking. Zico, Falcao, Junior, Socrates — I'll never forget them, and nor will Brazil. Bernd Schuster, the West German who for some reason argues with Beckenbauer, has class. So, too, has Hagi, the Rumanian. So much like George Best, so unlucky not to play in the 1986 World Cup Finals. Graeme Souness and Ray Wilkins

France feel the power of Bryan Robson, as the England skipper fires past 'keeper Jean Luc Ettori after just 27 seconds of their 1982 World Cup game.

Can you become the longest serving England captain?

Robson: I'll have to go some to overtake Bobby Moore and Billy Wright. Bobby did the job 91 times in 108 games between 1963-73 and Billy captained England on 90 occasions in 105 appearances.

Yes, I've taken on Kevin Keegan, who led out England in 31 games, and have captained the country more than Emlyn Hughes (23) and Johnny Haynes (22).

It's always a good quiz question to ask people to name the two goalkeepers who have captained their countries to World Cup success. There have been two: Dino Zoff, for Italy, in 1982 and Combi, for Italy, way back in 1934.

Which England goal has given you most pleasure?

Robson: That first goal of three England scored against France in the 1982 World Cup Finals. It came in 27 seconds. I can remember thinking as that ball went in the net 'we can win the World Cup'.

What's your idea of a good day off?

Robson: Get up at 9.00; read the papers; go for a swim with the kids; have a good lunch, maybe a lager at the pub run by former Scotland and Manchester United star Pat Crerand.

The future?

Robson: I never think about it. I just thank my mam and dad for all the encouragement they gave me when I had no idea I would one day captain England and Manchester United. I've loved every moment, playing a great sport.

CONTINUED

are two of the best midfield men of my time. I haven't seen too many players to match Trevor Francis. That pace, it could kill you off.

There are others — Peter Shilton, Pat Jennings, Ray Clemence; Alan Hansen, Mark Lawrenson, Paul McGrath; Liam Brady in his Arsenal days; Frank Stapleton, Terry Butcher, Mark Wright, Gary Lineker, Glenn Hoddle. I shall never forget what Mark Hateley did for England's World Cup qualification in 1986. Kenny Dalglish, Paul McStay, Ian Rush and Mark Hughes. Gordon Strachan, Peter Barnes, Jesper Olsen ... oh the list is endless. Cyrille Regis has a place in my heart from our West Brom days. And if I said John Wile, my old teammate at West Brom, I'd know that those who've followed the fortunes of Albion will accept what I'm saying. All special players in my mind.

Mark Hateley hammers England's first goal against Finland in a World Cup qualifying tie at Wembley in October, 1984. He scored again in a 5-0 rout.

Emeka Nwajiobi, Luton's talented Nigerian chemist, is one of the modern game's enigmas. Signed from Dulwich Hamlet, the highly educated striker is just as much at home with a test tube. But his form for David Pleat's team of entertainers has been a revelation ... and a headache. "You never know what he is going to do next," admitted Pleat: "and I can see why some players tear out their hair trying to predict him. But he's a gem for the fans."

OSMAN'S ENGLAND DREAM

Russell Osman's career was made! Ipswich were riding high he partnered Terry Butcher at the heart of their defence and England wanted him. But it all went horribly wrong for the defender in a series of England games in which other players of superior experience flopped — leaving the luckless Osman to help carry the can. Butcher went on to World Cup glory but Osman had to change clubs to rekindle his career. He took the bold step in July 1985, joining Leicester City under Gordon Milne ... and quickly became a favourite with the Filbert Street fans: "I had to make the break," he said: "I was sad to see that fine Ipswich team break up but you cannot lose the likes of Paul Mariner, Alan Brazil, John Wark, Arnie Muhren, George Burley and Eric Gates and carry on challenging for major honours."

Raw deal

Osman, who won 11 full caps before the disasters of defeats in Switzerland and Norway caught up with him, believes he got a raw deal: "I won more caps after those awful games, but suddenly I was out of the reckoning. Yet I had a great partnership with Terry and it could have been a great success for England." Now, Osman is reminding us of the form that first won his international spurs and made him one of the best central defenders in the game. City's gain is without question Town's loss.

15

Manage a laugh

"They're gonna write home and tell my mum and dad about me."

"In view of our unfortunate habit of missing open goals — I've devised this new training scheme."

"Meet our new 'keeper, coach!"

"Not only does it toughen their muscles, boss — it also rolls the pitch."

WHAT A SEASON! OUT OF BOTH CUPS AND EUROPE AS WELL!

BOTTOM OF THE LEAGUE AND NOT A WIN SINCE CHRISTMAS

WILL THIS CLUB EVER WIN ANYTHING?

DON'T DESPAIR! THERE'S THE MANAGER OF THE YEAR 'TO BE NOMINATED YET!

16

BIG HEAD ... Arsenal defender Viv Anderson wins this midair battle against Mike Trusson of Rotherham in last season's F.A. Cup Fourth Round tie.

The most exclusive club in Britain

The Millionairos

*T*ransfer fees have plummeted since Manchester United splashed out £1.5 million on Bryan Robson to shatter the British record.

But if Britain's managers were given the freedom to spend, spend and spend again with an open cheque-book, which of today's players would command transfer fees in the £1 million bracket?

We introduce you to a special breed of golden talent...

BRYAN ROBSON

'I'd play for nothing'

Bryan Robson has already figured in one £1 million deal and would clearly persuade any ambitious manager to bust the bank again to capture the services of the Manchester United and England star.

Ron Atkinson broke the British transfer record when he splashed out £1,500,000 to shift Robson from West Bromwich Albion to Manchester United in October, 1981.

Since that transfer coup, Robson's career has accelerated to dizzy proportions.

He served notice of his world class status for England in the 1982 World Cup by scoring a goal in just 27 seconds against France.

It took new England manager Bobby Robson no time to recognise Robson's leadership qualities and almost half of the England star's first 50 international appearances were as captain.

He led England to the 1986 World Cup Finals and has starred in all Manchester United's trophy winning exploits since his arrival at Old Trafford.

More important than his contribution to the United trophy cabinet is that Bryan Robson has proved himself to be a truly world class player in an era when superstars are a rare breed.

The Italians know what Robson is worth even if the modest superstar shrugs off much of the acclaim he receives.

"I'd play for nothing. I love the game that much," he says.

PAUL McSTAY
Scotland skipper

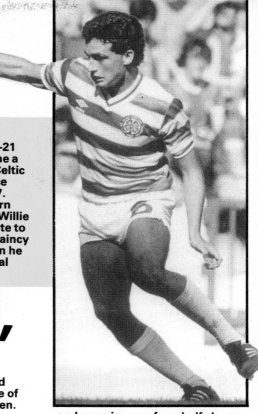

A product of the prolific Celtic Boys' Club, Paul McStay has risen from that nursery to become the Rolls-Royce of Scotland's midfield.

His 5ft 10in frame, lean and well muscled, glides classically through the Parkhead mud for Celtic to revive memories of former golden midfield generals.

He broke into Scotland's team in 1984-85 and became a prominent member of the national side in the 1986 World Cup Finals.

A former Scotland Under-21 international, he has become a permanent fixture in both Celtic and Scotland midfields since turning professional in 1977.

Still only 21, Hamilton born McStay, brother of Celtic's Willie McStay, is a strong candidate to take over the Scotland captaincy from Graeme Souness when he retires from the international arena.

IAN RUSH
'Killer'

Ian Rush's phenomenal goal-scoring for Wales and Liverpool has made him one of Europe's deadliest marksmen.

No British striker has commanded greater respect on the Continent than the 6ft 2in hitman Rush.

He served notice of his goal-scoring ability when Liverpool forked out £300,000 to sign him from Chester in May, 1980.

Since then he has featured heavily in all Liverpool's trophy winning exploits.

No players has been marked more heavily than Rush in recent seasons, but his electrifying pace and unerring eye for a half chance have left defenders for dead.

He forms a lethal goal-scoring combination with Mark Hughes, and it was through no fault of theirs that Wales failed to qualify for the 1986 World Cup.

Rush, PFA Player of the Year in 1984, has outstripped or kept pace with leading First Division strikers ever since winning a first team place at Liverpool.

That 'killer' instinct around goal propels him into the £1 million bracket as a bargain!

NORMAN WHITESIDE
Wembley winner

Norman Whiteside has accomplished more in five years at Manchester United than some players do in a lifetime.

He has played in two World Cups for Northern Ireland and enjoyed the distinction in the two F.A. Cup Final appearances he made against Brighton and Everton in 1983 and 1985.

All that by the age of 20.

His rapid development after being discovered by the legendary Manchester United scout in Northern Ireland, Bob Bishop, has sent his name into the record books.

In playing for Northern Ireland in the 1982 World Cup, Whiteside became the youngest player to take part in the Finals. Who did he succeed? None other than Pele!

But Whiteside has risen into the £1 million bracket only since departing from his striking role in favour of withdrawn duties on the left side of midfield.

It was from a midfield position that he picked up the ball to crack the winner against Everton in 1985.

If he ever became available, many of the Europe clubs would leap for his signature at £1 million plus.

Norman wins the F.A. Cup for Manchester United in 1985.

BLISSETT'S ENGLAND

When it comes to taking on the world in boots, nobody has more first-hand experience than Watford's former England striker Luther Blissett.

The Jamaican born forward, who progressed through the Vicarage Road Juniors to turn professional in July, 1975, has spent his career proving an army of carping critics consistently

'Being dumped shattered me'

wrong.

As he thundered in goals during Watford's promotion march from Division Four in 1978 the 'experts' predicted he would struggle to keep up his prolific finishing in the higher division.

But Blissett kept it up all the way through the League until The Hornets celebrated their debut season in Division One as runners up to Liverpool in 1982-83!

"I suppose they were fed up being proved wrong for a while," says Blissett: "but those same critics were back when I started playing for England.

"I actually hit a hat-trick in only my second game as we crushed Luxembourg 9-0 at Wembley. Did I hear the popping of Champagne corks? No, I heard people whining about the chances I'd missed that night.

"I decided then to ignore it once and for all. What more can a man do in this game?"

Graham Taylor.

When Italian club AC Milan handed Watford a £1 million for Blissett in the summer of 1983, he left his beloved Watford watery-eyed but determined to make the grade abroad.

"I grew up out there. I was alone, on and off the field, and homesick. But I gave them my all. They expected me to wander about up front on my own, get the ball at my feet then take on the tightest, hardest defenders in the world game.

"I only scored five goals in 30 games during my stay and people claimed I was done for, found out,

BLAST

etc. But I sharpened my skills, toughened up and when Watford brought me home a year after selling me I repaid them with 28 goals in my first season back.

"Manager Graham Taylor kept telling me to ignore the snipers and carry on doing what I was best at — scoring goals. But it broke my heart when, after being told how well I'd played against Russia at Wembley, despite a 0-2 defeat, I then discovered that my international career was over after 14 caps.

"Nobody bothered to tell me. I worked it out all by myself because I was ignored. Manager Bobby Robson didn't say a word, not even 'You won't be needed any more.' I don't expect to be thanked or anything like that. But it wouldn't hurt for the manager to tell a player he no longer figures in plans.

"That gutted me and my form went to pieces. The manager rested me, rebuilt my confidence and I bounced back in scoring form ... only to shatter my knee cap in a fluke accident against Leicester that ended my interest in season 1985-86 half-way through.

"Now I'm back again, scoring goals and, touch wood, free of critics. But in this game those critics are hard to please. If you are not careful you can go onto the pitch carrying them on your back. I nearly did but I play for a quality manager and he is the only one I have to please."

WHEELER

Forced to operate on a shoestring yet they've turned small clubs into giants.

Hand a fairly average League club manager a cheque for £5 million and the freedom to go out and buy any player he fancies in the world and the chances are that he will build up a highly successful team after recovering from the shock of receiving the handsome gift.

Complete freedom to buy more or less who they like gives Liverpool's Kenny Dalglish and big spending Manchester United boss Ross Atkinson a golden opportunity to keep their teams high and mighty in the Championship stakes.

Money is no object either at Spurs, Arsenal and Everton, who use their bulging bank balances to splash out large sums on some of Europe's finest players.

But what of the lesser clubs and the men who run their playing affairs on a shoestring?

In many respects these managers, forced to wheel and deal and confined to the small provincial town clubs of England, deserve greater credit than they receive.

Some say they are the *best* in the game.

Money doesn't make Kenny Dalglish a better manager than Ken Brown, the Norwich City manager who has built several highly successful teams in his time running the proud East Anglian club.

Can Ron Atkinson, free to bid and buy anywhere he likes, count himself a better boss than David Pleat, the Luton Town chief?

It is perhaps significant that the last two England managers have been plucked from the homely confines of two of the First Division's smaller outfits.

Ron Greenwood strode proudly into F.A. headquarters from West Ham, and Bobby Robson sharpened the talents that were to lead to Lancaster Gate from the cold, windswept wastes of East Anglian Ipswich Town.

They were considered to be the best managers available at the time of their appointment and neither had had an opportunity to spend millions in the transfer market.

Has there been a better manager in Britain since the War than Brian Clough?

Clough, often tipped to take control of England but never allowed to do the job for fear that his unconventional attitude would upset officialdom, has spent big money, very big money in his association with Nottingham Forest since January 1975.

But most of the time he has been forced to build teams on a limited budget.

The heyday of rocketing transfer deals, which saw Forest spend a record £1,250,000 on Ian Wallace (Coventry) in July 1980, and indulge in other staggering transfers involving Trevor Francis and Justin Fashanu, has given way to more restrained Cloughie management.

Many would argue that the old warhorse has been at his most astute since tucking the cheque-book in his back pocket and concentrating on building star players from spotty faced newcomers.

It is a long time since Forest won the European Cup twice in 1979 and 1980, yet even since the financial constraints were imposed on Clough's regime he has kept his Forest side in strong contention for all the major trophies without making anything like the same impact in Europe that they had at the end of the Seventies.

The rise of Nottingham born defender Chris Fairclough, Peter Davenport, his own son Nigel, and Franz Carr testify to the skills of a Clough now relying mainly on player judgement than any big business transactions.

David Pleat is another giant at a little club. Luton Town's prominence

Above: Graham Taylor.
Left: David Pleat.

DEALERS!

since Pleat took over the reigns at Kenilworth Road in 1978 is a tribute to his undeniable flair.

His record in the transfer market is just as good as Brian Clough's. One of his shrewdest buys is England centre-half Steve Foster, snapped-up from Aston Villa for just £70,000.

Ricky Hill, Brian Stein, Mick Harford, Foster; Peter Nicholas (Wales); Mal Donaghy (N. Ireland); Ashley Grimes (Republic of Ireland); and Nwajiobi (Nigeria) are all better players for Pleat's special brand of soccer knowledge and ability to motivate everyone on his staff.

Taylor for England

It is no surprise that Graham Taylor has been frequently tipped to manage the England national team.

Again, he has impressed the FA hierarchy with his ability to succeed in management at a club run on a tight budget.

He showed his spurs in steering Lincoln to the Fourth Division title in 1976 and it was only a matter of time after arrival at Watford that they should take-off into the big time.

Division Three runners-up in 1979,

Division Two runners-up in 1982, Division One runners-up in 1983 illustrates the rapid strides Taylor made at Watford.

He will readily admit the debt he owes club Chairman Elton John, but Taylor embodies so many of the strengths English football needs if it is to recapture its pride.

Taylor relies heavily on flair, ambition, plain commonsense, loyalty to his players, and a clear sight of what he is trying to achieve.

He is certainly not a 'win at all costs' merchant.

To Graham Taylor, the game of football is almost more important than the prize. He wants to carry off the trophies as much as the next man, but there is a quiet dignity about the way this man works, something that many other managers could do well to emulate.

Lawrie McMenemy, boss of Sunderland, is another proud member of this elite gallery of managers.

He hardly had a bean to spend at Southampton, yet turned a small but proud team going nowhere into one of

Forest's Peter Davenport (centre) and Brian Rice (left), testify to the skill of a Brian Clough no longer able to pay big fees for players.

the First Division's most formidable sides.

He took them to the 1976 F.A. Cup Final and watched proudly as they beat Manchester United to lift the Cup. They were League Cup runners-up in 1979 under his command — again with a necessary penny-pinching campaign that saw Southampton reach heights previous regimes had often contemplated but never accomplished.

Lawrie McMenemy was very much a big fish in a 12 year reign. He thought big, acted big, and bagged big headlines for his club.

They came no bigger than they did when McMenemy's charm and ambition lured Kevin Keegan back into First Division football.

He could have gone to Manchester United, Arsenal, Chelsea or Everton — but he chose Southampton. The Lawrie McMenemy charm school had worked a treat.

Given pots of money to spend and the freedom to run one of the big city clubs, it is mind-boggling to consider what Messrs. Clough, Pleat, Taylor and McMenemy would achieve.

Maybe, they are happier where they are.

Giants in their own right.

*Above: Brian Clough.
Right: Lawrie McMenemy.*

IDENTICAL

Which two pictures are identical?

NEVILLE SOUTHALL.   PAUL McGRATH.   IAN RUSH.
(Everton)   (Man. U.)   (Liverpool)

BIRTHPLACE

Unscramble the letters to find the birthplaces of these three players.

PUZZLE

SOCCER SEARCH

B	L	O	O	M	F	I	E	L	D
B	I	R	M	I	N	G	H	A	M
V	V	V	A	R	A	D	I	I	A
K	E	N	B	R	O	W	N	C	I
E	R	A	B	E	R	D	E	E	N
E	P	A	U	N	A	M	R	X	E
P	O	R	T	S	M	O	U	T	H
E	O	A	T	G	S	S	E	R	A
R	L	R	O	W	H	E	L	A	N
S	T	E	V	E	N	S	A	D	D

*Below are listed a number of clues, the answers to which can be found spelt out **Down** or **Across** only in the square of letters. Draw a line around each of these answers and when you have done this in every case there will be 12 letters which you have not used. These letters (reading across and travelling downwards) will spell the name of an English First Division club's ground.*

(1) Gary —, Spurs midfielder. (7)
(2) Remi —, of Man. United. (5)
(3) — City, The Blues. (10)
(4) Norwich City manager. (3 & 5)
(5) St. —, Scottish club. (6)
(6) Imre —, WBA striker. (6)
(7) Bruce Grobbelaar for instance! (6)
(8) — Road, Blackpool's ground. (10)
(9) Pompey is their nickname. (10)

(10) Gary —, Everton defender. (7)
(11) — Road, home of Man. City. (5)
(12) Ronnie —, Liverpool midfielder. (6)
(13) — -time is played in Cup-ties. (5)
(14) Scottish Champions in 1984-85. (8)
(15) — -ball is not allowed. (4)
(16) They won the European Cup in 1984. (9)
(17) The —, of Derby County. (4)

SIGNED-UP

Study the autograph and the clue and identify the player.

He established himself as a full-back for Celtic last season.

TIME

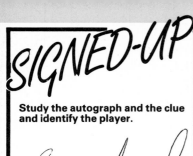

ROBINSON'S ROUTE

Help Bryan Robson find his way to goal without meeting a defender.

ANSWERS ON PAGE 125

MYSTERY MAN

Who is this world class striker and which club does he play for?

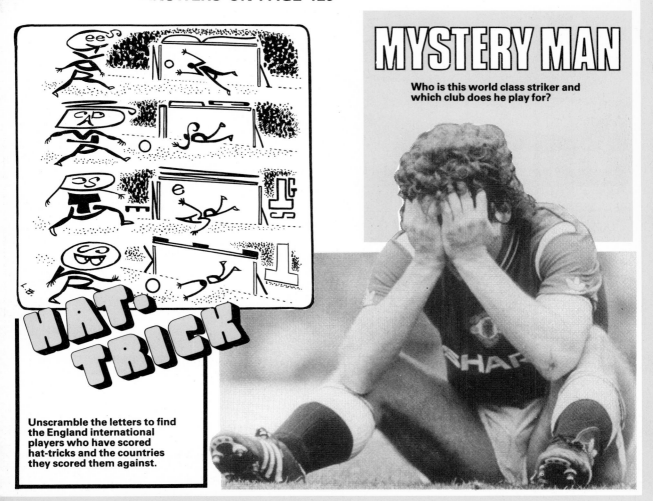

HAT-TRICK

Unscramble the letters to find the England international players who have scored hat-tricks and the countries they scored them against.

Singing Canaries after beating Sunderla[nd] in the 1985 Milk Cup Final.

Canaries crack Wembley jinx

When Norwich lifted the Milk Cup in 1985 it was a case of third time lucky.

The Canaries had been to Wembley twice before in the competition's pre-sponsorship days when it was known simply as the League Cup.

Ron Saunders was the City boss when they were beaten 1-0 by Tottenham Hotspur in 1973. And two years later, when Norwich had John Bond at the helm, Saunders saw his new club, Aston Villa, triumph by the same scoreline.

But all that was forgotten on Sunday, March 24, 1985, when Ken Brown's boys defeated Sunderland 1-0 to give the Carrow Road club their biggest-ever trophy success.

Norwich did win the old-style League Cup in 1962 with a two-leg defeat of Rochdale but the competition was in its infancy and snubbed by the major clubs who didn't think it had a future!

In 1907, when The Canaries were still members of the Southern League, they produced one of the biggest shocks in FA Cup history by beating holders Sheffield Wednesday.

Just one year later Reading objected

Record run . . . then saved from extinction!

to the size of City's ground, The Nest, and their FA Cup clash was switched to Stamford Bridge.

The tie went to a second replay at Villa Park which Norwich won and they went on to beat Liverpool at Anfield before their Cup campaign was ended by Bristol City.

In the 1950's, by which time their present Carrow Road ground had been opened, Norwich claimed some famous FA Cup scalps.

In 1951 they eliminated Liverpool for the second time and three years later went to Highbury and dumped the mighty Arsenal out of the competition.

Stunned

But it was in 1959 that their Cup exploits stunned the whole of football. Manchester United, Cardiff City, Tottenham Hotspur and Sheffield United were all beaten before The Canaries lost to Luton Town in a Semi-Final replay.

And that record run came just two years after the club almost went out of business due to a financial crisis which was averted by the launching of an appeal fund!

Manager Brown's double

Norwich boss Ken Brown joined an elite group when he led The Canaries to a memorable Milk Cup triumph in 1985.

Mick Channon (left)...one of manager Ken Brown's shrewdest signings.

Dave Watson

He became one of a select band of football personalities who have been Wembley winners as players and managers.

Ken was centre-half in the West Ham United side that defeated Preston North End in the 1964 FA Cup Final.

Watson's shock move

Skipper Dave Watson has been worth his weight in gold to Norwich.

He was still a teenager when he moved from Liverpool in 1980 in a £50,000 deal. But his value soared as he established himself at Carrow Road and graduated to international status.

There were no complaints from Norwich when they had to fork out a further £50,000 after he had completed a specified number of appearances.

Or when they had to send an extra £100,000 in the direction of Anfield after

Dave's debut for England in the historic 2-0 defeat of Brazil in the Maracana Stadium during the summer of 1984.

Scouser Dave, a regular on the Kop as a youngster, had been a sheet metal worker before becoming a full-time professional. And Liverpool had to think twice before letting him go.

Indeed, as Dave recalls, his transfer to Norwich was a surprise for everyone concerned.

"They were interested in Colin Irwin," he remembers, "but after seeing a reserve game they switched their attention to yours truly.

"It was a wrench to leave Anfield at the time because I had high hopes of making the grade there. But I got my chance in the First Division and with England because of Norwich so I have no regrets."

Dave, who also won seven England Under-21 caps, was Brown's first signing for the club. He took over as captain following the departure of Northern Ireland international Martin O'Neill to Notts County in the summer of 1983.

Meanwhile, back at Anfield, another member of the Watson clan is being tipped for the top.

Younger brother Alex, an England youth cap, is reckoned to have a bright future.

A matter of fact

● Norwich City were founded in 1902. Three years later they turned professional and were elected to the Southern League. They were founder members of Division III (South) in 1920 and in 1935 moved to their present Carrow Road headquarters.

● Their amazing record of 23 draws in 42 League games during the 1978-79 season was the highest-ever since the Football League was founded.

● Norwich have twice sold players for £1 million. Kevin Reeves went to Manchester City in March, 1980, and in August the following year Justin Fashanu moved to Nottingham Forest.

● Fire destroyed the main stand at Carrow Road in October, 1984, wiping out the dressing rooms, Boardroom and guest lounges. The club lost many valuable items of memorabilia.

● Back in the First Division as 1985-86 Champions of the Second Division, Norwich will be aiming to improve on their best ever League position ... 10th in the First in 1975-76.

MAGIC AND

Football can thrust a player to the heights — and cast him into despair. Four stars talk about contrasting moments of joy and heartache.

PHIL THOMPSON
Sheffield Utd

MAGIC: As a local lad, it was marvellous to be signed as an apprentice with Liverpool, rub shoulders with my schoolboy heroes, and become one of the select few to become a first team regular. Along with Phil Neal, I hold the record for the number of Championship medals won with the club — a magnificent seven.

MISERY: I must hold the most unwanted record at Anfield for the number of injuries I sustained and which blocked me from gaining even more honours with the club. My injury list would match that of someone run over by a steamroller: two cartilage operations; a broken wrist; chipped ankle bones; torn ligaments; broken collarbone; broken nose (twice). And then when I was on loan to Sheffield United — a great club — I suffered a collapsed lung.

MAGIC: Being made captain of my country ranks as my biggest international thrill. And it came about by accident! A friendly against Bulgaria had been fogged off at Wembley. Captain Kevin Keegan couldn't stay for the rearranged game on the Thursday, as Hamburg needed him, and manager Ron Greenwood staggered me by saying: 'You're captain of the League Champions, Phil, so you take over.'

MISERY: It was a real sickener not reaching the 1982 World Cup Semi-Finals at least in Spain. We only conceded one goal and it was cruel luck that left us goalless against West Germany and Spain.

Phil Thompson was staggered when told he was to captain England at Wembley.

Last season was misery for West Brom's Steve Hunt (stripes).

STEVE HUNT
West Brom

MAGIC: Signing for New York Cosmos in the North American Soccer League and playing alongside World-famous stars, such as Pele and Beckenbauer, was a tremendous thrill. I was with them for two seasons in the late Seventies and returned for another season in 1982, and collected three Soccer Bowl Championships medals. I learnt more from those stars than from any coaches.

MISERY: Last season was the most depressing I've ever experienced. We had such a lot of quality players, yet couldn't get our act together and struggled from start to finish. A real downer.

MAGIC: I really thought I was making the start of a long run for England when I came on as substitute at Hampden Park against Scotland in 1984. The football wasn't too different from that at club level. The pace was quicker and it suited me. We ended up with a 1-1 draw.

MISERY: My next appearance was again as a sub, this time against Russia at Wembley. Whereas I knew most of the Scots side, the Russians were complete strangers and knowing nothing about them did make it difficult. We lost 2-0. I got into the squad against Turkey, but sat on the bench as England won 8-0. Then Manager Bobby Robson dropped me — and it's still a mystery why!

MISERY

PAUL STURROCK
Dundee Utd

MAGIC: Being part of the first Dundee United side to take the Premier Division Championship flag is something that will thrill me forever. It was a real cliff-hanger of an ending to the 1982-83 season, when we needed to take both points in a match against our neighbours Dundee. We won 2-1. It meant that at last we ranked alongside the very top teams in Scotland and became a force to be feared.

MISERY: It still hurts to recall the disgraceful way we crashed out of the European Cup competition in 1984. We'd played our hearts out in the first-leg of the Semi-Finals at home to Italian club Roma, and went to Rome with a 2-0 lead. At least eight of us — including me — hardly put a foot right on the night and the Italians justly thrashed us 3-0 to go through to the Final with Liverpool!

MAGIC: I scored my first goal for Scotland in a World Cup qualifier against Portugal in Lisbon. But unfortunately we lost 1-2, and no one in Britain saw my goal because of a strike by Portuguese TV people. But I'll never forget that strike by me!

MISERY: No one but another professional footballer knows how soul-destroying it is to have to pull out of playing in a game through injury. It's murder sitting around waiting for it to mend and also worrying about whether your place is in jeopardy.

Paul Sturrock (second left) helped Dundee United to their first Top Ten title.

Peter Beardsley made his England debut against Egypt.

PETER BEARDSLEY
Newcastle Utd

MAGIC: Being a Geordie, what greater thrill could I have than sign for Newcastle United. I'd started my career with Carlisle, then had two spells with Vancouver Whitecaps, with a period at Manchester United between, and it was marvellous to find myself at St. James' Park. Football's a strange game, you just never know what fate has in store.

MISERY: My greatest disappointment was not getting a single League game with Manchester United. I've nothing against the club. The fact is, the team had such a great run — getting into two Cup Finals and finishing third in the League — I just didn't get the opportunity to show what I could do.

MAGIC: To appear for England on my first time in the squad has to be marvellous. I got on the field for the last 35 minutes in the World Cup warm-up against Egypt. We won 4-0. I was a bit annoyed that the Press tended to concentrate on Peter Shilton's great performance in goal. The other players performed just as well.

MISERY: I can't say that so far I've had anything to complain about when it comes to playing for England. I know it'll hit me really hard when the day comes I don't get the call!

Most footballers have the same schoolboy admiration for superstars from other sports that young signature hunters have for their professional game.

The greatest living sportsman for most footballers in the past 20 years has been the former World Heavyweight Champion Muhammad Ali.

Boxing's King was the public's favourite throughout the Sixties and Seventies — and hardly a footballer in the land failed to respond to Ali's ring magic.

Ali's special brand of hype 'I shall float like a butterfly, sting like a bee' sent him soaring to the top of opinion polls reflected by

FOCUS MANIA

Muhammad Áli
A big hit with our top stars

Shoot's highly popular weekly series 'Focus'.

"Favourite other sportsman?" posed Focus. No hesitation. No other candidate. All the soccer stars supported Muhammad Ali.

Today, Ali is not forgotten and never will be. He is a legend. But a host of other world superstars have risen in the ranks of their various sports to win the hearts of the modern stars.

Boxing has never quite found anyone to replace the 'Greatest', but Sugar Ray Leonard's brief but explosive career shot him to favour and Marvellous Marvin Hagler has a host of admirers this side of the Atlantic.

Barry McGuigan, the 'Clones Cyclone', is likely to remain one of Britain's favoured sons for several years, but since Ali departed the scene other sports have had a chance to improve their Focus ratings.

Chelsea's Scottish striker David Speedie admires the fluent running of Olympic Champion Sebastian Coe.

Speedie, who spends a lot of time wielding a camera when he is not scoring goals for Chelsea, has yet to capture Coe on film but cannot disguise his admiration for the great athlete.

"Unlike most athletes," says Speedie, "Seb has always managed to bounce back after injury to silence his critics."

Speedie's top player from the world of football is not British!

He's French star Michel Platini.

"Quite simply," says Speedie: "Michel has got the lot."

Portsmouth forward Vince Hilaire likes nothing better than to go home from training, put his feet up in front of the fire, and open a book.

Not any old book. Hilaire is a student of cricket and has worked his way through a host of books on the summer game.

Right: The player's Champion Muhammad Ali on his way to victory over Britain's Joe Bugner.
Below: Gordon Greenidge is Vince Hilaire's favourite.

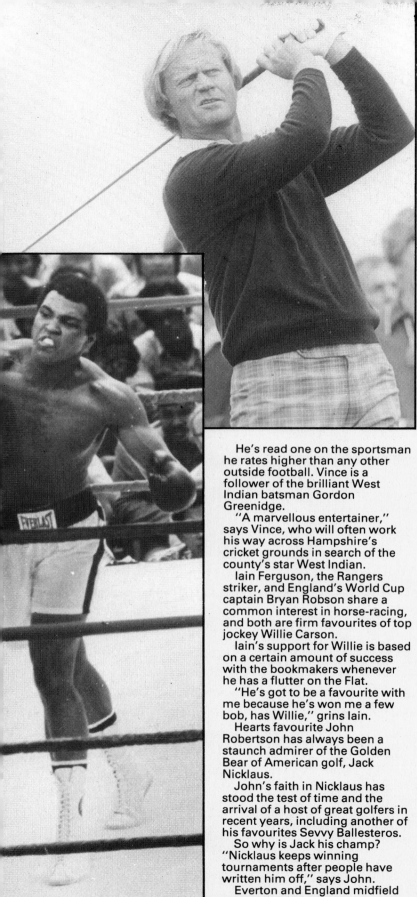

Olympic colossus Daley Thompson for no other reason than 'Daley is a superb all-round athlete'.

Sheffield Wednesday forward Brian Marwood declares a dead-heat when asked by 'Focus' to name his favourite from other sports.

He goes for top Ryder Cup golfer Sandy Lyle and wonder athlete Steve Cram.

"They have done so much for British sport," says Brian.

Billy Hamilton, one of the most popular players to come out of Northern Ireland, cannot be shifted from backing one of his fellow countrymen.

Left: John Robertson is a fan of Jack Nicklaus.
Above: Trevor Steven had no hesitation naming Daley Thompson as the sportsman he admires most.

He's read one on the sportsman he rates higher than any other outside football. Vince is a follower of the brilliant West Indian batsman Gordon Greenidge.

"A marvellous entertainer," says Vince, who will often work his way across Hampshire's cricket grounds in search of the county's star West Indian.

Iain Ferguson, the Rangers striker, and England's World Cup captain Bryan Robson share a common interest in horse-racing, and both are firm favourites of top jockey Willie Carson.

Iain's support for Willie is based on a certain amount of success with the bookmakers whenever he has a flutter on the Flat.

"He's got to be a favourite with me because he's won me a few bob, has Willie," grins Iain.

Hearts favourite John Robertson has always been a staunch admirer of the Golden Bear of American golf, Jack Nicklaus.

John's faith in Nicklaus has stood the test of time and the arrival of a host of great golfers in recent years, including another of his favourites Sevvy Ballesteros.

So why is Jack his champ? "Nicklaus keeps winning tournaments after people have written him off," says John.

Everton and England midfield star Trevor Steven is a self-confessed admirer of Britain's

No doubt in Billy's mind. His vote goes to Barry McGuigan, the BBC's Sports Personality of the Year in 1985 on the strength of his World Championship exploits.

Guess who Scotland winger Pat Nevin goes for. Not Viv Richards, the West Indian Test star. Not Daley Thompson. No, not Alain Prost, from the world of motor racing, or top Jocky Steve Cauthen.

What about John McEnroe? Not, he's not a favourite either.

Pat Nevin, often described as a 'thinking footballer' with a string of academic qualifications to match his wizardry on Chelsea's wing, has a Champion few Shoot readers have ever heard of.

Pat's choice is Jim Morrison. Jim who?

Says Nevin: "Jim Morrison, a basketball player from Scotland".

Today, tomorrow, next year new favourites will win the approval of our top soccer stars, but none of them will ever forget the impact that Muhammad Ali made in our Focus columns all those years ago.

All go for Mighty

Ask the country's top defenders to nominate their most dangerous opponent and one name is certain to be well to the fore.

Even if the question was asked of players on both sides of the border the answer might be the same — mighty Mo Johnston!

The blond striker terrorised defences in England following a £200,000 move from Partick Thistle to Watford and he has continued in the same vein since his £400,000 return to Celtic.

It was Mo's brilliant record of 40 goals in just 85 League appearances for his first club, Partick Thistle, that persuaded Watford boss Graham Taylor to take the plunge.

The gamble paid rich dividends. Mo was The Hornets' leading marksman in the 1983-84 season with 24 goals — not bad considering he didn't move South until after more than a quarter of the fixtures had been completed.

He started with a double blank as Watford, just three places off the bottom after finishing runners-up the previous year, lost to both Manchester United and Luton.

But a hat-trick in the 5-0 annihilation of Wolves earned Johnston instant fame and he reaped a harvest of 20 League goals before the end of the campaign to haul his team to mid-table respectability.

Another four goals helped steer Watford to a first-ever FA Cup Final appearance. They lost the Wembley showdown with Everton 2-0 but it was a memorable day for the homely Hertfordshire outfit who, just a few years earlier, seemed trapped in the lower reaches of the League set-up.

Home sick

But Johnston's stay at Watford was punctuated with as many trips home to Scotland as goals. And eventually the club agreed to let him move on with less than a quarter of his contract completed.

The player got his wish of a transfer to Celtic, the club he had supported since childhood. And Watford brought a smile to their bank manager's face by charging twice as much as they'd paid for him just 11 months earlier.

In just 38 League games for the Vicarage Road side Johnston had scored 23 goals and the fans flooded into Parkhead to see his debut in the famous green and white hoops of his new club.

Again the scoring statistics were impressive. His 27 League appearances produced 14 goals and a further five were scored en route to Hampden Park where he helped Celtic defeat Dundee United to lift the Scottish Cup.

At international level, too, Johnston has regularly been among the goals. His debut was as a substitute against Wales when, typically, he fired the winning goal in Scotland's 2-1 success.

And not even the ruthless defending of Spain could stop him grabbing a brilliant double in a vital 3-1 World Cup qualifying victory that steered the Scots a step nearer Mexico.

Still only 23, Johnston can look forward to many more years of goalscoring at the top level for both club and country.

That's good news for followers of Celtic and Scotland.

Left: A hero for Scotland ... Mo heads Scotland's second goal in their fine 3-1 victory against Spain in the World Cup at Hampden. Above: A hero for Watford ... with former team-mate George Reilly after beating Plymouth in the 1984 F.A. Cup Semi-Final to reach Wembley.

Mo

THE THINGS THEY SAY ABOUT ...
STEVE PERRYMAN

One cap wonder

We study the career of one of the game's outstanding personalities through the things that have been said about him by friends and rivals.

CHARLIE FAULKNER, the scout who spotted Steve Perryman for Spurs in 1966:
"I first saw Steve when he made his debut for Ealing Schoolboys. He was only a tiny tot but covered acres of ground and had ability to go with his enthusiasm. I knew he had great potential and tried to talk him into signing for Spurs, but he wanted time to think things over because Arsenal, West Ham and his local club Queens Park Rangers were also interested. I kept a close watch on him for a year and knew I had pulled off a great coup for Spurs when I persuaded him to come to White Hart Lane."

BILL NICHOLSON, who as Spurs manager gave Perryman his League debut at the age of 17 in 1969:
"Steve has never been frightened of responsibility and will tackle any job without complaint. I used to worry when he first came into the side that he would burn himself out but he has learned to pace himself and knows when he can afford to coast. He performed wonders for Spurs."

EDDIE BAILY, who was Spurs coach when Steve made the breakthrough into the first-team:
"Steve has got a good football brain and a heart that is bigger than his head. His energy is just unbelievable and he puts many of his team-mates to shame with his effort."

MARTIN PETERS, the England star Perryman succeeded as Spurs captain:
"I can never understand why Steve has not been a regular in the England squad. He has the same qualities as Nobby Stiles used to have. He is a

marvellous competitor who is always on the go and demanding the same total effort from the players around him. When things are going against you it's reassuring to look up and see Steve working away like a beaver. He has a great competitive streak in him and will never admit defeat until the final whistle."

KEVIN KEEGAN, former England star who played with Perryman at Under-23 level:
"Steve was outstanding as a teenager and I would have put money on him establishing himself as a regular in the full England team. He is a 100 per center whose lack of real speed never

caused him to be exposed. It's a mystery why he never won dozens of caps."

OSVALDO ARDILES, his team-mate at Tottenham and speaking after skipper Perryman had led Spurs to the F.A. Cup Final victory over Manchester City:
"It has been a privilege for me to play with Steve on the pitch and to be a friend of his off the pitch. He has always made me feel at home and I have a great respect for his ability."

BOBBY ROBSON, who gave Perryman his one and only England cap when he sent him on as substitute against Iceland in 1982:
"Steve was good enough to have won many more caps but for a variety of reasons he didn't get the opportunities he deserved. I was delighted to give him the chance of collecting a cap so that he has testimony to his talent."

GRAHAM ROBERTS, his partner in the Spurs defence:
"Steve is one of the most inspiring players in the League. He lifts everybody around him with his incredible energy and enthusiasm and encourages us all to give extra effort."

MICK CHANNON, who has played against Perryman many times in League matches:
"There is not a forward in the First Division who does not respect Steve Perryman. He is a very hard player but he is always fair. I can't say it's a pleasure to play against him because he makes life hard for you."

PETER SHREEVE, Tottenham manager who gave him a free transfer in March 1986:
"Steve was a magnificent servant for Spurs. You can mention him in the same breath as Dave Mackay and Ron Burgess, two former idols of the club. Any young professional just starting out in the game could not do better than follow his example. He will do a good job for Oxford United."

The gamble that worried Ipswich manager Bobby Ferguson has paid off! Ferguson paid Derby County £150,000 for Kevin Wilson in January, 1985 and spent the rest of season 1984-85 fretting about his investment.

But by the time the curtain had come down, Ipswich were safe from the relegation that threatened them for most of the campaign and Wilson's splendid return of seven League goals in 17 games was largely responsible.

Banbury born Wilson was in the thick of another relegation battle in 1985-86, but by then he was an accepted hero at Portman Road where many fans quickly forgot about the sale of Eric Gates to Sunderland as Wilson twisted and turned defences with pace and skill.

"I took my time settling down because I kept changing partners up front," said Wilson.

"When I arrived from Derby I had an established record as a striker. But the manager put me on the bench and played Alan Sunderland, Gates and Mich D'Avray. The fans began chanting my name which made me feel embarrassed.

"Injury to Sunderland gave me my chance and I grabbed it. I'd wanted badly to play in the First Division. And although I played a few games there

WILSON SAVED IPSWICH

with Derby, by the time I'd settled into their side they were relegated!

"That's why I felt less pressure than most when Ipswich went through their transition and fight for survival."

Wilson's finishing, experience and willingness to help the kids around him made him an invaluable asset to Ferguson as he blooded more and more youngsters.

"I settled down to playing alongside Mich D'Avray and we were the ideal duo.

"He has the height, the aerial power and the strength to make a superb target man. I played off him and

Mich D'Avray (left) found his form when Kevin Wilson arrived from Derby County.

35

between us we gave the best defences in the League plenty to worry about.

"The lad is gentle by nature, but he really worked to add steel to his game for the sake of the team. He became a better player for it and improved his scoring rate.

"Me? I kept buzzing round the box and grew more confident as the goals started to flow.

"I have never seen so many talented young lads as we have at Ipswich. Teenagers like Mark Brennan, Jason Dozzell, Ian Cranson and Nigel Gleghorn are on the verge of becoming First Division household names and this team can emulate the great F.A. Cup and UEFA Cup feats of recent years.

"People moaned when the stars were sold — Wark, Mariner, Gates, Burley, Osman, Muhren and Thijssen. Well they have a whole new crop to cheer now!"

PETER SHILTON
Southampton

Mark Lillis
City crazy

Mark Lillis spent his childhood and youth praying that Manchester City would succeed. They went one better and signed him, from Second Division Huddersfield — the original fan-turned-star. "I was City crazy as a kid," he said: "And when I got the chance thanks to Billy McNeill, I was overjoyed." Lillis quickly established himself at Maine Road with powerful runs and vital goals as they recaptured First Division status.

NOT A LOT OF PEOPLE

Late, Late goal

STEVE Whitworth played in 569 Football League games for Leicester City, Sunderland, Bolton Wanderers, and Mansfield Town before scoring his first goal — a penalty for Mansfield v Hereford United, March 23rd, 1985. Steve scored a second penalty 11 days later.

Happy Birthday

LONDON born Tommy Langley, who played for Chelsea, QPR, Crystal Palace, AEK Athens, Coventry City and Wolves celebrated his 17th birthday in 1975 by scoring the winning goal for Chelsea v Birmingham City in a First Division game.

Denis the menace

DENIS Law, one of the greatest goalscorers in the game's history, amassed a total of well over 300 goals in Football League, F.A. Cup, League Cup, major European competitions and Scottish internationals. Considering that this wizard of the goal area scored most of his goals for Manchester United it is quite an ironic coincidence that the final first-class goal of his career was for Manchester City in a 1-0 win over United which sent them down into the Second Division in 1974.

Flu off

IN April 1974 Exeter Ciy refused to play a Football League fixture at Scunthorpe. Nine of their players had 'flu but the Football League would not agree to a postponement. Exeter were fined £5,000 and ordered to pay £1,000 compensation to Scunthorpe United. The Lincolnshire club were also awarded two points for a game that was never played. Three weeks later Exeter beat Scunthorpe 4-0 at St James' Park.

Revenge!

IN November, 1984 Partick Thistle were beaten 7-3 at home by St.

DENIS LAW

Johnstone in a Scottish First Division game. In their next meeting just over three months later on the same ground Partick beat St Johnstone 6-2. Only five of Partick Thistle's players played in both games.

First sub

Although substitutes were not officially permitted in the F.A. Cup unitl 1966 it is reported that the first to appear came on for Hyde United against Preston North End way back in 1887. This was the game which Preston won 26-0, and as they were already 12 goals up when Hyde introduced their substitute centre-half. Preston

obviously didn't think it worth while complaining.

Hot-shot Cooke

IN 1984-85 Robbie Cooke was top scorer for both Cambridge United and Brentford. He had scored six goals for Cambridge before he was loaned to Brentford in December (he was eventually transferred in March). When the season had ended Robbie had netted 12 for The Bees to finish joint top scorer with Keith Cassells.

Hot-shots Oldham

THE only club to have run up a double-figure score in more than one post-war Football League game is Oldham Athletic. In 1951-52 they beat Chester 11-2 in Division 3 (North) — including seven goals from centre-forward Eric Gemmell — and in 1962-63 they beat Southport 11-0 in the Fourth Division — Herbert Lister scoring six goals.

Flash trick

ON January 1st, 1983 Brian Stanton scored four goals for Huddersfield in a 6-3 Third Division victory over Bradford City, including three goals in six minutes. This is one of the fastest hat-tricks ever scored by a midfield player.

FANtastic

IF you believe that the record attendance (including any replays) for the Scottish F.A. Cup Final was for one of the clashes between those great rivals Rangers and Celtic you would be wrong. The record was created in 1948 when Rangers beat Morton 1-0 in a replay after a 1-1 draw.

St. Johnstone 'keeper Gordon Drummond fails to stop John Donnelly putting Partick ahead at Firhill Park in November, 1984...sensational Saints won 7-3!

KNOW THAT...

Above: Scotland's Steve Archibald weaves through England's defence at Wembley in May, 1981.
Right: Tony Coton made a fantastic debut for Birmingham City.

The aggregate attendance of these two games was 262,746. This is nearly 13,000 more than the aggregate of the two games between Rangers and Celtic in the 1963 Final.

Eurocrats

NO British player has yet succeeded in scoring double figures in a single European Cup competition. The nearest to this target were Dennis Viollet (Manchester United) with nine goals in 1956-57, and Denis Law (Manchester United) with the same total in 1968-69. The European Cup record aggregate for a single season is 14 by José Altafini (AC Milan) in 1962-63. That was the first season in which the Final was played at Wembley and Altafini scored both of his side's goals in a 2-1 victory over Benfica.

Wembley woes

IN the 114 years of international football England has only once played more than two games in succession without scoring and that was as recently as 1981. Then a goalless draw with Rumania was followed by a 0-1 defeat by Brazil; a goalless draw with Wales and a 1-0 defeat by Scotland. All these games were played at Wembley!

Super saver

AT the age of 19 goalkeeper Tony Coton made one of the most sensational First Division debuts with Birmingham City in December, 1980. Not only did his side enjoy their first victory in six games, beating Sunderland 3-2, but Tony saved a penalty less than two minutes after the kick-off. Tony was transferred to Watford in September, 1984.

Four goal loser

ONE of the keenest goalscoring tussles of recent years was the Third Division game between Doncaster Rovers and Reading in September, 1982. Rovers were leading 5-3 at half-time and won 7-5. Glynn Snodin scored a hat-trick for the Rovers (including two penalties) while Kerry Dixon got four of Reading's goals, including one penalty. Not many players have scored as many as four goals yet ended on the losing side.

13 years without a game

PETER Knowles was on Wolverhampton Wanderers' books for 13 years without playing a single game! A colourful character, Peter was a goalscoring inside-forward who made 163 League appearances, scoring 58 goals, between 1963 and 1969. Then on the verge of international honours he shook the footballing fraternity by announcing his retirement from the game at the age of 23 to work full-time for the Jehovah's Witnesses. Wolves did not tear up his registration until 1982. Peter's brother Cyril had a full career of over 400 League games with Middlesbrough and Spurs.

Wigan Wondermen

IN April, 1979 Wigan Athletic were 3-0 down in a Fourth Division game at home to Port Vale but scored five in the last 25 minutes to win 5-3. Peter Houghton netted a hat-trick for the winners.

Rich Rochdale

FOURTH Division Rochdale have the lowest income of all the 92 League clubs. But are in the black because of thriving off-field activities.

NEIL WEBB
Nottingham Forest

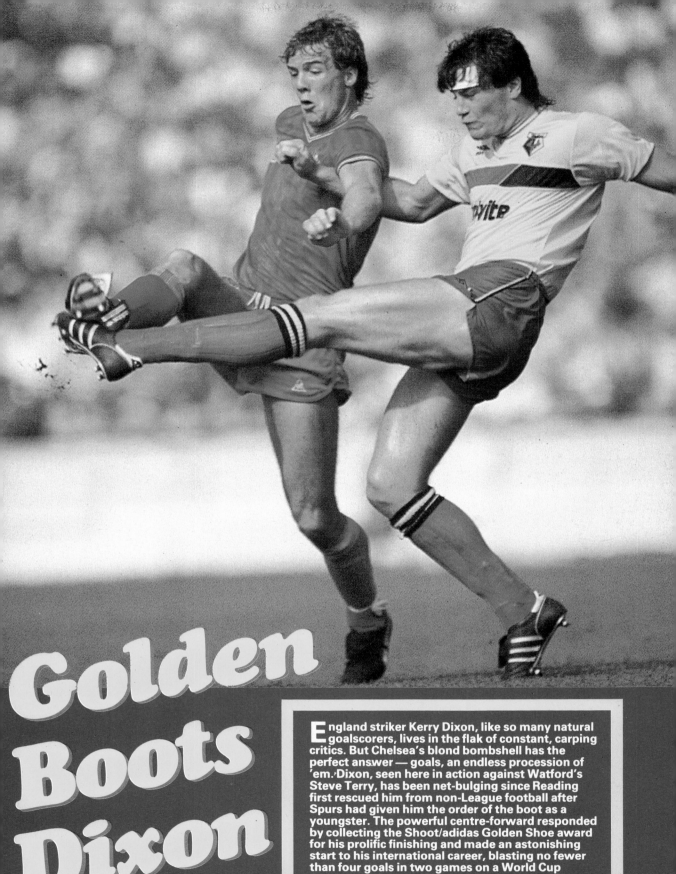

Golden Boots Dixon

England striker Kerry Dixon, like so many natural goalscorers, lives in the flak of constant, carping critics. But Chelsea's blond bombshell has the perfect answer — goals, an endless procession of 'em. Dixon, seen here in action against Watford's Steve Terry, has been net-bulging since Reading first rescued him from non-League football after Spurs had given him the order of the boot as a youngster. The powerful centre-forward responded by collecting the Shoot/adidas Golden Shoe award for his prolific finishing and made an astonishing start to his international career, blasting no fewer than four goals in two games on a World Cup preparation jaunt to Mexico and the United States.

CUP MAGIC
SPELLS GLORY
TH

There is nothing that brings out the glorious uncertainty of our game more than a sudden death Cup competition.

What is it that enables a non-League team of part-timers to strike the form to beat a full professional side?

How is it that in Cup-ties Third or Fourth Division clubs sometimes find something extra to beat a top First Division side? Are these victories flukes?

The Giant-killers would refuse to accept such an explanation and they would be right to do so. Most of these surprises have been pulled off on merit.

What became of Manchester United as recently as 1983-84?

They were placed second to Liverpool in the First Division yet a Milk Cup defeat by Third Division Oxford United was followed less than three weeks later by a 2-0 F.A. Cup defeat at Third Division Bournemouth!

True, Oxford were top of the Third Division, but Bournemouth were three places off the bottom and had won only three of their previous 11 League games.

Indeed, in the previous round they had struggled to beat Windsor & Eton 2-0 at home after a goalless draw at Windsor. Yet in the game at Dean Court the mighty United were shattered by two goals in two minutes with Milton Graham and Ian Thompson scoring in the 60th and 62nd minutes.

Arsenal's amazing crash at Walsall in the F.A. Cup way back in 1933 is still regularly recalled in stories about Cup "Giant-killing," as is Yeovil Town's 2-1 victory over Sunderland in 1948-49, but games not so frequently mentioned are Boston United's 6-1 win at Derby County in 1955-56 or Hereford United (then in the Southern League) beating

Harlow hero Neil Prosser after 90th minute goal earned the li non-Leaguers a replay at Leice City.

Q.P.R. 6-1 in 1957-58. Admittedly the losers were Third Division clubs at the time but no 6-1 win could be described as any kind of fluke.

Midland League Boston United were managed by former Derby player Ray Middleton and included no less than five ex-Rams in their side. That may have been part of the explanation for this shock result.

FOR GIANT-KILLERS

Milton Graham scores Bournemouth's first goal against mighty Manchester United.

Derby's only goal was scored from the penalty spot. It was Derby's first home defeat of the season.

Only the previous Saturday they had beaten Darlington 6-2 at the Baseball Ground. Cup magic indeed, and the biggest-ever win by a non-League side on a League club's ground in the F.A. Cup.

Isthmian League Bishop's Stortford enjoyed a bit of Cup magic in the F.A. Cup Third Round in January, 1983 when they came back from 2-0 down to draw 2-2 at Middlesbrough. True, Second Division Middlesbrough won the replay 2-1, but why couldn't they have polished the minnows off at Ayresome Park?

In January, 1980 when Leicester City were heading for promotion to the First Division, and hadn't lost any of their last seven home League games, Isthmian League Harlow Town came to Filbert Street in the F.A. Cup, Third Round.

Leicester went a goal up before the interval through Martin Henderson, but only three minutes from time Neil Prosser (later with Bournemouth) snatched an equaliser.

Never mind, Leicester would win the replay easily. Not likely, Harlow beat them 1-0.

In the next round Watford, whom Leicester had already beaten twice that season, k.o'd Harlow at Vicarage Road, but what a fight they put up before going down 4-3.

There is Cup magic in Scotland as well as south of the border.

Like in January, 1967 when Berwick Rangers beat Rangers 1-0 with Sammy Reid hitting the historic goal.

That was the Glasgow giants' first-ever defeat by a club from a lower division and the first time in 30 years that they had been beaten in the First Round.

More recently Second Division Forfar Athletic enjoyed a Cup run in 1981-82 during which they caused a major upset by winning 1-0 at Hearts.

Then, after beating Queen's Park 2-1 they held Rangers to a goalless draw in the Semi-Finals at Hampden Park. Rangers needed to pull out all the stops to defeat them 3-1 in the replay.

Perhaps an even bigger shock happened in 1983-84 when Premier Division Hibernian were eliminated by Second Division East Fife who held them to a goalless draw at Easter Road before beating them 2-0.

However, in the next round Celtic hammered The Fifers 6-0 at Bayview Park. But that was magic of a different kind.

Despite Hibs pressure, East Fife (stripes) won the glory in a tense tie at Easter Road in January, 1984.

Fearless Frank

The secret of Aberdeen's tremendous success in the Scottish Premier Division has been manager Alex Ferguson's ability to sell stars and replace them without disrupting the team's performances. One such replacement is Frank McDougall, signed from St. Mirren in the summer of 1984. He stepped into the number 9 shirt vacated by Mark McGhee, sold to Hamburg, and was an instant hit with the Pittodrie fans. Strong, fast and brave, McDougall fears nobody in his pursuit of goalscoring opportunities. At the end of his first full season, 1984-85, McDougall blasted 26 League and Cup goals and collected a League Championship medal as well as finishing top scorer. Frank added the Shoot/adidas Golden Shoe to his collection of honours. Today, Scotland hails him as 'Fearless Frank'!

NICKY MORGAN
Portsmouth

SCOTLAND

likely candidates for the 1990 World Cup

SCOTLAND were unbeaten in the 1974 World Cup Finals in West Germany ... they nosedived amid a flurry of sensational drug-taking accusations in Argentina '78 ... Brazil blitzed them in Spain '82 and they just made Mexico '86.

One way or another, the Scots have been a headline-writer's dream come true with their performances in four successive World Cup Finals. They have never been far from controversy and in West Germany, Argentina and Spain contrived to fail to get through their early sections on goal difference!

Already, though, the Scots are assembling a new tartan force, preparing for the World Cup Finals in 1990, rearing fresh-faced youngsters to take on the ultimate soccer challenge in three years' time.

Extrovert Tommy Docherty, never slow to alert anyone to the country of his origin, says in a defiant tone: "Scotland is second only to Brazil in unearthing genuine, quality soccer players."

And a few superb individuals have arrived on the scene from that particular conveyor belt. Names such as Denis Law, Jim Baxter, Kenny Dalglish, Jimmy Johnstone, Billy Bremner, Joe Jordan, Graeme Souness and so on immediately spring to mind.

But who are the up-and-coming kids who are going to carry on the good work? Who are the superbabes ready to take on the world in 1990?

The Rock

What a delight Chelsea's wily, winger Pat Nevin will still be around to use the '90 World Cup Finals as a platform upon which to parade those devastating skills.

And his Stamford Bridge colleague Joe McLaughlin could be the rock in the Scottish rearguard by the time the 1990 World Cup Finals come round.

Ball-playing Gary Gillespie, so unlucky with injuries at Liverpool after his £300,000 transfer from Coventry three years ago, is another who could be vying for a spot in central defence — although regular No. 5 Alex McLeish, of Aberdeen, is adamant he will still be doing his stuff on the right side of 30 in three years' time!

His Pittodrie team-mate Neale Cooper, whose versatility has proved to be so valuable to Aberdeen in recent seasons, will, barring disasters, also be a

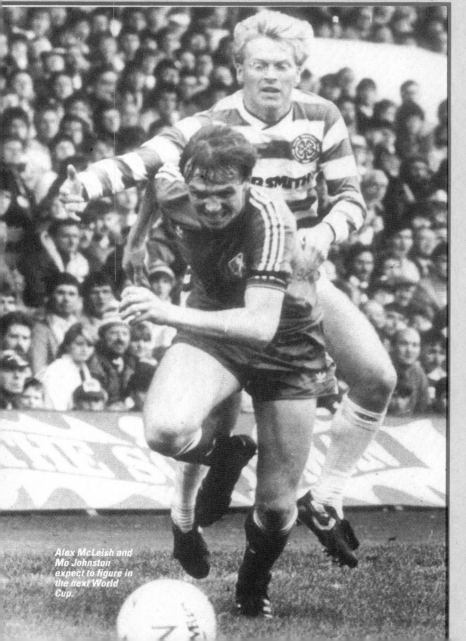

Alex McLeish and Mo Johnston expect to figure in the next World Cup.

ON THE MARCH

Rangers fans have been excited by the skills of young Derek Ferguson (left).

attackers who threaten the Edinburgh club's goal.

Three other baby-faced defenders who are destined to make life a misery for opponents are St. Mirren's Stevie Clarke, Dundee Tosh McKinlay and Motherwell's Fraser Wishart.

And who will be the last line of defence? The Scottish goalkeeper's position has been abused so much in recent years that it could be re-named the laugh line of defence!

But the reliable Jim Leighton has put a halt to the smirks and snide comments— mainly from South of the border! — and his Pittodrie understudy Bryan Gunn, Rangers' Nicky Walker, St. Mirren's Campbell Money and Dundee United's Billy Thomson could be the men putting on the pressure for the No.1 jersey.

mainstay on the international scene.

The ferocious, blond-haired, no-nonsense Cooper, born in India where his father worked on a tea plantation, can play in the back-four and midfield with equal distinction and he will revel in the big-time.

Another Aberdeen-raised player who has the ability to terrorise foreign defenders is the magnificent Eric Black, whose talent in the air has got to be seen to be believed.

And a player who knows all about his style courtesy of their days together in the Under-11 team is Brian McClair, one of Celtic's most consistent marksmen.

Of course, a certain Charlie Nicholas, who will be a mere 27 in 1990, will also be hoping to be strutting the international arena again and his friend Mo Johnston, who missed out in '86, will hardly be a veteran by then.

But their places up front will certainly be under attack and whizz-kid John Robertson is another intelligent, gifted raider who possesses that in-bred quality of always being in the right place at the right time in crowded penalty areas.

Helping Nevin keep a steady stream of passes to the firing squad could be Dundee United's elegant Kevin Gallacher and the equally-skillful Owen Archdeacon, of Celtic.

The blinding talents of Paul McStay demand an international

stage and it could be that Celtic have the players to present a complete midfeld trio for the international side!

Peter Grant, so full of industry, and Tony Shepherd, so full of invention, are two well-groomed youngsters who continually put outsize smiles on the face of the Celtic faithful.

Roy Aitken could be father of

Campbell Money could put pressure on Jim Leighton.

the Celtic kids in the Scottish arena — at the ripe old age of 30.

Davie Cooper was the lone Ranger to make the Mexico trip, but the Ibrox fans have been encouraged by the startling talents of two ball-artistes in their midfield, Ian Durrant and Derek Ferguson.

Hearts could also provide some engine-room power in the shape of Gary Mackay, one of the most under-rated youngsters in Scottish football, but a player who pulls many of the strings at Tynecastle.

And while Mackay fires them up in midfield, tall, talented Craig Levein devours lack-lustre

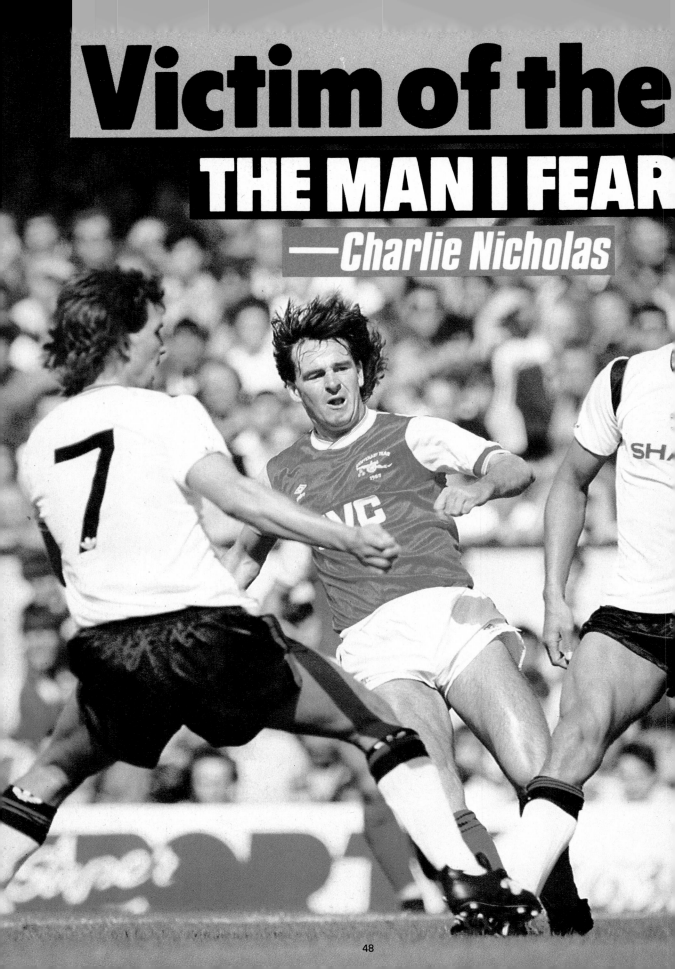

Victim of the
THE MAN I FEAR
—Charlie Nicholas

Gentile touch

MOST!

Only one man has ever succeeded in putting the fear of God into me. That man was Claudio Gentile.

The former Italian World Cup winner is without doubt the hardest and most fearsome opponent I've ever faced.

The last I heard of him, he was playing for Atalanta and by all accounts he's still kicking forwards all over the place. Mark Hateley and Paul Rideout deserve every lira they're reportedly earning if they have to face that sort of punishment every week.

I'll never forget the night I became a victim of the Gentile Touch. I was playing for Celtic, he was playing for Juventus and we met in a European Cup First Round tie at Parkhead.

I was a nervous 19-year-old playing in my first European match. Signor Gentile certainly opened my eyes!

I'd been warned he was the sneakiest, most ruthless defender in the world. It was all true — and worse.

It was a simple case of anything goes. He elbowed me in the face, punched me in the back and in the ribs, pulled my hair, kicked me from pillar to post and even spat at me.

But the man who went on to earn a World Cup winners' medal the following year against West Germany was such a master of his art that the ref didn't spot a thing.

Golden rule

I'd always been brought up never to let an opponent put me off my game and to never retaliate. I failed on the first count and to this day don't know how I resisted the temptation to break tha second golden rule.

Ironically, the toughest defender I've faced in British football was a team-mate.

I'm referring to Celtic's Roy Aitken, whose strength and speed in training made him absolute murder to get past.

The lads called him 'Shirley Temple' because of his golden curls, but there is nothing soft about big Roy. We might have been on the same side on Saturdays, but during the week he'd think nothing of giving you a kick if he thought it was merited in training.

Since joining Arsenal, I'd say the king of the First Division hard men is Manchester City's Mick McCarthy.

I remember our game at Maine Road last season when the midfield became so congested we started to hit long, high balls ino the box.

McCarthy is built like a collosus and is as strong as an ox. He was brea-

thing down my neck all game and trying to hold him off was no joke.

The secret of getting the better of Mick is to let him get side on to you then try to turn him quickly. But once we started pumping them into the air, I didn't get a look-in.

But the best header of a ball in the First Division has got to be Manchester United's Paul McGrath — no giant compared to most stoppers but almost unbeatable in the air.

United have often played Paul in a midfield role, but I reckon he's much more effective in the middle of the defence because he consistently wins so many important headers.

He is also one of the best tacklers around, although he does have a tendency to go through you to get to the ball at times.

McGrath has got to be one of the top defenders in football today, but my vote for the best all-rounders would go to the Liverpool duo of Mark Lawrenson and Alan Hansen.

Strong in the air, tremendous in the tackle and quicker than any other defenders I've ever faced, these two are pure dynamite.

Even if one of them makes an error, the other is always on hand to clear the danger. I'm certainly not the only First Division striker to have had no joy out of these two.

Mark Lawrenson and Alan Hansen are everthing good defenders should be. And something Claudio Gentile could never be!

Gentile by name . . . but not by nature. The Italian World Cup star is the terror of Europe.

You are the REF

2

MY BALL. LEAVE IT!

As a high ball drops into the penalty-area a defending player shouts out "My ball — leave it." Do you: (a) award a penalty, (b) an indirect free-kick, or (c) allow play to continue?

1

An attacker deliberately stoops and brings a challenging opponent down. Do you: (a) wave play on, (b) award an indirect free-kick, or (c) award a direct free-kick?

3

A trainer runs on to the pitch without your permission to attend one of his players. Should you: (a) allow this, or (b) order the trainer off the field?

5

The manager of a team shouts instructions to his players from the sideline. Should you: (a) caution him, or (b) ignore him?

4

You extend time to allow a penalty to be taken. The kick is saved, but the kicker follows up and shoots the ball into the net. Should you allow the goal?

ANSWERS

1. Award a direct free-kick (c). This constitutes a tripping offence. 2. Award an indirect free-kick (b). The player must call a name in order not to deceive an opponent. 3. Order the trainer off (b). He should also be cautioned as he must have your permission before entering the field of play. 4. No. Play is only extended for the taking of the kick. Once the keeper has made the save the game is over. 5. Caution the manager.

KEVIN RATCLIFFE
Captain Everton and Wales

One thing big money has done to the game is to reduce the number of players who stick to a single club throughout their professional careers.

Fortunately there are still a few players around today who have remained loyal to their original club and resisted the temptation of a bonanza.

The first professional to set a standard for club loyalty was Bob Crompton the Blackburn Rovers full-back who created an England record for appearances in the Home International Championship which was not broken for 44 years. He was a professional with the Rovers for over 23 years up to May, 1920.

This record of service was broken by Ted Sagar, one of the all-time greats among goalkeepers, who was an Everton player for just over 24 years until retiring in 1953 when he had made a club record 465 League appearances which stands to this day. His total would have been higher but for the intervention of World War II.

Before the War there were other loyal servants like goalkeepers Jerry Dawson and Tim Williamson — 22 years with Burnley and 19 years with Middlesbrough respectively.

Full-back Alex McNair played for Celtic for 21 years, while winger Alex Smith was with Rangers for the same length of time.

Dougie Gray, another full-back, surpassed Smith's record for Rangers by serving them for 22 years up to 1947, making a Scottish record total of 879 appearances, 801 in League and Cup.

Since the War there have been a number of really outstanding players who preferred to remain with one club.

Winger Tom Finney put in 23 years with Preston North End. Just think of

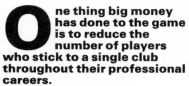

Jackie Charlton ended his long Leeds career on a high note.

ONE CLUB Soccer

DANNY McGRAIN

it. The average player considers himself lucky if he can stay in the first-class game for ten or 12 years, but rarely remaining with one club.

Only one year behind Finney are Roy Sproson (Port Vale), Billy Liddell (Liverpool), Sam Bartram (Charlton Athletic) and Joe Shaw (Sheffield United).

One of England's finest skippers, Billy Wright, served Wolves for 21 years, the same length of time with a single club as three other England internationals — Jimmy Dickinson (Portsmouth), Jackie Charlton (Leeds United), and Gil Merrick (Birmingham City), as well as Bob McKinlay, Nottingham Forest's central defender who was an ever-present when they fought their way back to the First Division for the first time since the War in 1957.

Don't think that all of these players just faded away, hanging on after their usefulness had passed.

Billy Wright, for instance, retired when still at the peak of his profession, winning a League Championship medal in his last season when he missed only three League appearances, and those, remarkably enough, because of international commitments.

Yes, this Wolves star played nine times for England in his final season! Those were great days at Molineux!

Others who ended long careers on a high note were Tom Finney, who made 37 First Division appearances and was Preston's top scorer with 17 goals in the final season before hanging up his boots at the age of 38; Sam Bartram rounded off his career with 33 appearances, Joe Shaw 27, and Jackie Charlton 18, all of these in the First Division.

Looking at the lists of registrations for the 1985-86 season we find only six players with over 16 years service with a single club — three either side of the border.

Among those in the Football League it is perhaps significant that

during 1985-86, his 17th season on the payroll at The Hawthorns. He was actually on their books for an earlier season as an amateur.

A Scot who joined the Albion straight from school Ally is by no means the only Scot in recent years to devote his entire career to an English club.

Another who immediately springs to mind is Eddie Gray who was 21 years with Leeds United until 1984.

Most famous of the three longest serving one club Scottish League players in 1985-86 is Danny McGrain who first established himself as right-back in the Celtic side in 1972-73, nearly at the end of their run of nine successive League Championships.

He immediately made such an impact that he was capped before the end of that campaign. In 1986 this outstanding defender completed 19 years at Parkhead.

WONDERS
oyalty can pay off!

ALLY ROBERTSON

the two longest serving one club players were both with London clubs — Steve Perryman with Spurs and Billy Bonds with West Ham. Next to them comes a Scot — Ally Robertson with West Bromwich Albion.

In the Scottish League we have Danny McGrain (Celtic), Hamish McAlpine (Dundee United) and Jim Fallon (Clydebank).

There has never been a more dedicated professional than Steve Perryman. Before his move to Oxford in March, 1986 he served Spurs for 19 years.

For the past 17 seasons he has proved to be one of the most consistent players in the Football League and was "Footballer of the Year" in 1981-82 when he lead his side to their second F.A. Cup win in successive seasons.

Tottenham's London rivals West Ham have a reputation for looking after their players. Only a couple of years ago Trevor Brooking retired after 19 years with the club, while another England international, Frank Lampard, completed 21 years at Upton Park before joining Southend as player-coach at the end of the season 1984-85.

Powerful central defender Ally Robertson was still battling away with luckless West Bromwich Albion

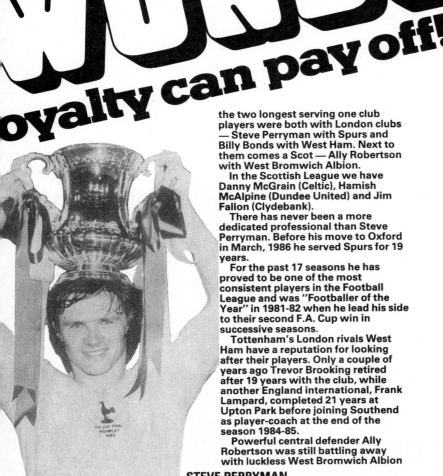

STEVE PERRYMAN

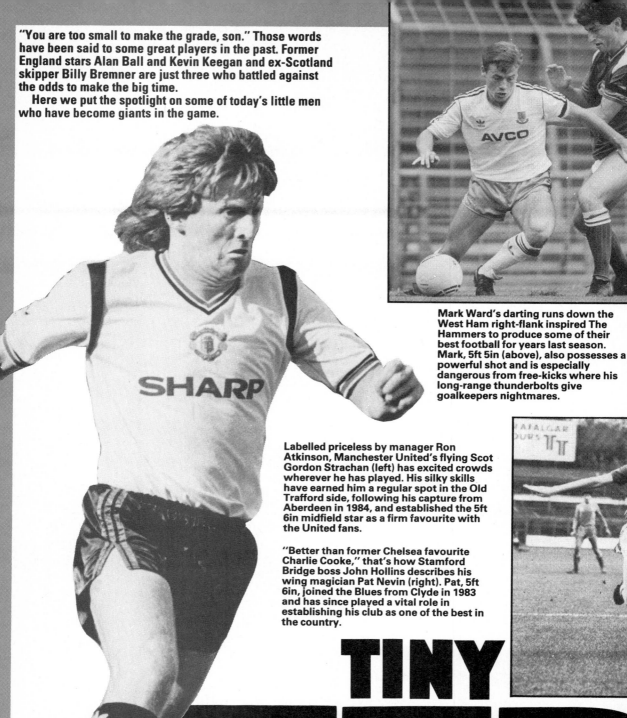

"You are too small to make the grade, son." Those words have been said to some great players in the past. Former England stars Alan Ball and Kevin Keegan and ex-Scotland skipper Billy Bremner are just three who battled against the odds to make the big time.

Here we put the spotlight on some of today's little men who have become giants in the game.

Mark Ward's darting runs down the West Ham right-flank inspired The Hammers to produce some of their best football for years last season. Mark, 5ft 5in (above), also possesses a powerful shot and is especially dangerous from free-kicks where his long-range thunderbolts give goalkeepers nightmares.

Labelled priceless by manager Ron Atkinson, Manchester United's flying Scot Gordon Strachan (left) has excited crowds wherever he has played. His silky skills have earned him a regular spot in the Old Trafford side, following his capture from Aberdeen in 1984, and established the 5ft 6in midfield star as a firm favourite with the United fans.

"Better than former Chelsea favourite Charlie Cooke," that's how Stamford Bridge boss John Hollins describes his wing magician Pat Nevin (right). Pat, 5ft 6in, joined the Blues from Clyde in 1983 and has since played a vital role in establishing his club as one of the best in the country.

TINY
TER

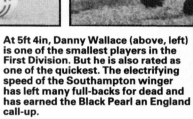

At 5ft 4in, Danny Wallace (above, left) is one of the smallest players in the First Division. But he is also rated as one of the quickest. The electrifying speed of the Southampton winger has left many full-backs for dead and has earned the Black Pearl an England call-up.

The old phrase 'have boots will travel', can certainly apply where Mickey Thomas (above) is concerned. The 5ft 6in Welshman started his career at Wrexham, left to join Man. Utd and then had spells at Everton, Brighton, Stoke and Chelsea before signing for West Brom in 1985. Mickey's tigerish aggression and enthusiasm for the game have earned him 50 caps for his country.

Adrian Heath (above, right) was on the verge of a full England cap when a knee injury put his career in doubt during the 1984-85 season. The 5ft 6in star missed Everton's success in the League and European Cup Winners' Cup but scored in his first game for ten months, a Charity Shield win over Man. Utd, and then regained his place in the Goodison Park side in a somewhat unaccustomed midfield role last season.

RORS

They aim to take Europe by storm...

When Howard Wilkinson was named Sheffield Wednesday's new manager in succession to Jack Charlton there was an air of anti-climax. Fans expected another big name. Instead, it was "Howard who?"

Now, just over three years later, Wilkinson is a Hillsborough hero and regarded as one of the top managers in the game.

Big Jack took the club out of the Third Division when Wednesday were at their lowest ebb. But it was Wilkinson who led them back to the First.

After two good seasons back in the elite Wednesday have the support, the finance — and the manager — to turn Hillsborough into another Anfield.

Chairman Bert McGee believes that Wilkinson and Peter Eustace are the men to make it happen.

"We want to be top of the First Division," he says. "And we want European football."

Wilkinson has made the sort of impact as a manager that he never made as a Wednesday player, back in the club's last First Division days of the Sixties.

After an unsung career as a winger, Wilkinson went into management with Boston United. Hardly the stuff of which Wednesday bosses are made!

Then, with Jimmy Sirrel, he helped Notts County to promotion

WEDNES WHIRL

Howard Wilkinson has earned respect the hard way.

Lee Chapman (right) regained his form at Hillsborough.

Glynn Snodin (light strip) was signed from Doncaster and made an instant impact.

DAY WIND!

when they're not doing it.''

In keeping Wednesday on the march, Wilkinson wants the club to walk before it can run.

''Our time back in the First Division has been a whirlwind,'' he says. ''The things that stand out are the disappointments, which is terrible — because that means one takes success for granted. More importantly, one hasn't taken time out to enjoy that success — and in years to come I think I'll regret that.''

What he doesn't regret is the punishing training regime that makes his run-all-day players among the fittest in the land — or the long ball style that's been widely condemned.

They've all heard of Howard Wilkinson now ...

Star striker Garry Thompson is given no special favours.

from Division Two. But even that achievement, and a job in the England set-up under Bobby Robson, failed to make him an appealing choice.

The 40-year-old Sheffielder has had to earn respect the hard way — and he has sought the same qualities from his players. Most are far from household names but have carved-out reputations under a boss who doesn't believe in lost causes.

Third choice

Howard's ''Salvation Army'' includes ... Brian Marwood, former Third Division winger, Martin Hodge, third-choice 'keeper at Everton before his move to Wednesday; Glynn Snodin, another from the lower Divisions who is tipped for international honours; Paul Hart, veteran centre-half freed by Brian Clough at Nottingham Forest; and Lee Chapman, the striker who was a £500,000 flop at Arsenal.

''I think the manager's secret is

that he goes into people's backgrounds,'' says Chapman. He checks to see if players are of good character and want to do well.

''I reckon it saves him a lot of money in the long run. I pride myself in that, even at Arsenal when things were going badly, I didn't buckle under. I always tried.''

Wilkinson has shown a willingness to exploit Wednesday's spending power but has never pandered to the wishes of his so-called star recruits. He bought Simon Stainrod and sold him within a few months.

Garry Thompson, his £450,000 record signing, also knows how difficult it is to command a place.

''It's nice to know someone can spend a lot of money on a player and not compromise themselves,'' he says. ''It helps keep you on your toes. It's good for me to know that I'm being given no favours. There's nothing more unsettling for other players than to see someone getting in

There was a time when Dundee were not only tops on Tayside but one of the giants of Scottish football.

When the Dens Park men were crowned Champions in 1962 their neighbours from across the road, Dundee United, were only just beginning to establish themselves in the First Division.

But in recent years the pendulum of power has swung in the direction of Tannadice with Dundee, albeit reluctantly, forced to play second fiddle.

While Jim McLean's 15 years in charge at United has seen them go from strength to strength, Dundee have seen several managers come and go without anything like the same level of consistency or success.

Now, however, there are definite signs that Dundee are on the way back. Former fan Archie Knox, whose playing career included a spell with United, is the new broom tipped to sweep the Dens Parkers back to the top.

Knox was previously Alex Ferguson's assistant at Pittodrie, where he did a sterling job in helping to establish The Dons in the forefront of European football.

John Brown a bargain buy from Hamilton Accies.

Dundee spending spree pays off

He would like nothing more than to do an 'Aberdeen' with his new club, whose solitary success since winning the title was in the old-style League Cup 13 years ago.

Knox has made many changes since taking charge, the most significant being an injection of fresh blood to reshape the senior squad.

The enforced departure of skipper Cammy Fraser and striker Iain Ferguson — they were at the end of their contracts and Rangers paid £400,000 for the pair — sent Knox on a shopping spree.

John Brown (Hamilton Accies), Tom Carson (Dumbarton), Robert Connor (Ayr United), Jim Duffy (Morton), John McCormack (St. Mirren), Stuart Rafferty (Motherwell) and Vince Mennie (Cologne) were all value-for-money captures.

But Brown, in particular, has proved to be worth his weight in

Master with the cheque book... manager Archie Knox.

gold. Although he's a midfield player, he can also operate at full-back and in the centre of the defence. And he's a more than useful goalscorer.

He was Dundee's leading marksman in his first season and his aggressive, determined style

typifies the positive attitude at Dens Park.

"Archie Knox is the best manager I've played under," admits Brown. "He tries hard to instil in us the high standards he obviously picked up at Aberdeen.

"I'm naturally grateful to him for giving me my big chance at the top level. I was with Hamilton for seven years and looking to progress. So the Dundee move was just what I wanted.

"There's a real feeling they we can go places. The Boss is absolutely determined to put the club on the map again and we have a squad of players capable of doing it."

Brown has already earned himself a place in the record books. In only his second season with Hamilton he scored three times in the 9-1 thrashing of Berwick Rangers — the first-ever hat-trick by a full-back in Scottish League history.

BRIAN STEIN
CARPET BAGGER

Brian Stein points to a carpet and a bagger as the reasons why he recaptured the form that earned him England honours.

Luton's striker, whose mercurial form waned after an exciting run partnering Paul Walsh, believes the sale of the blond cockney to Liverpool broke up a superb duo.

"But manager David Pleat put the club into the 21st Century with two strokes of his pen — he signed Mick Harford from Birmingham and gave the go-ahead for our all-weather pitch.

"The carpet is a dream to play on, brings out the real skills in players and gives you a true surface in all weathers.

"The bagger — an apt name for goal-bagging Harford — gave us power, height and immense strength and leadership in our attack. He upsets defences, scores goals, lays on chances for others and has tremendous skill for such a big man.

"I love playing alongside him. We experimented a lot with me playing back a bit behind a front two led by Mick, but either way our way of playing — running the ball through the team rather than belting it long, brought goals, excited crowds and established

Mick Harford has brought power and goals to Luton.

Luton as a top team and one of the most attractive outfits in England."

Born in Capetown, South Africa, Stein joined Luton from non-League Edgware Town and quickly established himself as a footballing striker with pace, a sharp turn and a fierce right foot shot.

In the League alone he marched past 300 appearances, scoring more than 100 goals — a superb one in three average.

Stein, who accepts that Luton will never rank among England's elite, feels strongly that the public should

not be misled into believing that you have to be in an imposing stadium such as Highbury, White Hart Lane, Old Trafford or Goodison Park to get value for money.

"We have a small, modest stadium and a hard-core support. But Town have brought through some of the most skilful players in the League — Ricky Hill, Mitchell Thomas, Mal Donaghy and Emeka Nwajiobi. Our manager demands good football and will not accept kick and rush.

"We have been blasted by him for winning without style and praised after losing certain games because we played with invention, courage and, as he enjoys, rampaging attacking with five and six men going forwards.

"Add the carpet and the bagger — and you can see why I'm happy to be a Hatter."

WHISTLE HAPPY

"Come here, you!"

"Might be an idea if you lifted him over the touchline — he's lying on the linesman."

"Rather unusual type of injury — dropped his whistle on the kneecap."

"Every time you dream you're sending someone off you always poke me in the eye."

"For the next pose — will you take me doing my famous two-fisted dive round the corner save?"

"Nope! I won't go until you apologise for sending me off."

"You told me to bring in anyone whose behaviour might cause a breach of the peace."

"I'd like to take this ball down to the station and have it tested for fingerprints."

GARY MACKAY has more reasons than most to hope Hearts are successful on match-day . . .

The elegant Under-21 international midfielder owns a pub a short corner-kick from Tynecastle!

"I like to go in and mix with the punters," says the blond-haired, long legged MacKay.

"There's no point in just turning up when you've played well and the team has won. You've got to show up when things haven't gone your way.

"You can take some stick at times, but it's all good-natured. I don't mind. As well as being a Hearts' player I'm a Hearts' supporter and I enjoy the banter with the men who are the very lifeblood of the game."

Hearts' fans were easily identified last season by their large smiles. They saw their team go to the top of the League for the first time in over a decade and there was a definite buzz in the air around Tynecastle.

Mackay's skill was appreciated by friend and foe alike and Alex Ferguson readily admits to being a fan of this intelligent young man who is the sheer epitome of a 100 per cent, 90-minutes professional.

"Sure, I like to give my all," says Mackay. "I'm not a cheat. Everyone at Hearts has the same outlook, believe me.

MacKay makes Hearts beat faster

"There's a great spirit about the place. It's Musketeers stuff. All-for-one and one-for-all stuff. It's marvellous to play in such an environment.

"I'm desperate to see Hearts attain a place right at the top. Not just for one season or two — but forever.

"This is a big club in every sense of the word. The potential is immense, we have great support and our millionaire chairman Wallace Mercer is always prepared to put money where his mouth is.

"And, of course, we've got Alex MacDonald and Sandy Jardine as our management team. They've seen and done it all at the top level and their attitude really motivates you."

Hearts' fans relish the thought of Gary Mackay taking over the mantle of one of their favourite sons, Dave MacKay, who made his senior debut with the Edinburgh outfit before going on to make an even bigger name for himself at Spurs in the Sixties.

"Yes, the older fans talk about Dave and tell me about all the wonderful things he could do," says Mackay. "But we're built along different lines and I don't think our styles could be compared.

"However, it's nice to know that you are mentioned in the same breath as such a magnificent professional as Dave Mackay."

FITNESS

DO'S Above all a 'keeper has to be as agile as a cat on hot bricks in order to reach high crosses, spring to make a save in the corner of his goal, and sprint off his line at the first sign of danger. Plenty of sprint work in training, combined with loosening-up exercises, is essential.

You must also be strong enough to stand up to physical challenges from human battering rams like Joe Jordan. Weight-training can help tone-up the body.

DON'TS Never go in for lifting heavy weights. This could make you muscle-bound and reduce your mobility.

POSITIONING

DO'S You must work constantly at discovering how to be in the right place at the right time. There are no hard and fast rules. For corners I prefer to position myself two yards inside the near post and about two yards off my goal-line. For free-kicks I place my human wall on one side of the goal while I guard the other.

DON'TS If you stand directly behind the wall you run the risk of being unsighted — until it's too late! And never place yourself right alongside the near post at corners.

HANDLING

DO'S One of the most important aspects of the game. You can be agile

Britain's most successful number one passes on the benefit of his vast experience. Budding 'keepers will learn a lot — and so will those on the firing line.

KEEP LIKE CLEM!

and brave, but if you can't catch the ball you can forget about making number one. When a high ball comes over, leap to catch it at its highest point. That way your hands should reach above any opponent's head.

Decide quickly whether you're going to catch the ball or punch it. Continental 'keepers are great punchers, but I regard it as a last resort simply because you can never be sure where the ball's going. Finally, get your body behind the ball whenever possible!

DON'TS I forgot that golden rule at Hampden Park in 1976 when England were playing Scotland, and I rate it amongst my worst Clemence clangers. Kenny Dalglish shot from close in. The ball went through my hands, and then between my legs and into the goal.

Another important tip is to avoid falling on your elbow with the ball, as the shock wave can knock it from your grasp.

Above: Catch the ball at its highest point. Right: In a one-against-one situation spread yourself as large as possible.

KICKING AND THROWING

DO'S Practise accuracy before working at getting distance. A quick fly-kick or throw to a team-mate after the opposition have pushed up too hard can start a deadly counter-attack.

DON'TS Never take your eye off the ball no matter how much pressure you're under. And don't pass to a team-mate with the opposition breathing down his neck!

PENALTIES

DO'S This is a situation where you have nothing to lose. All the pressure is on the penalty-taker. I often try to make him even more up-tight with a bit of gamesmanship to delay the kick.

I prefer to stand in the centre of the goal unless I've been told the kicker tends to go for a favourite spot. Generally it's best to make a guess as to which way to dive.

DON'TS Don't look defeated. Grin like Bruce Grobbelaar. And always move, one way or the other, when the kick's taken. I hate seeing a 'keeper rooted to his line with his arms flapping.

CONCENTRATION

DO'S It's harder to keep your mind on the game when you're behind a good side that's doing all the attacking. But you must remember you may only be called upon for ten seconds in 90 minutes — and then you've got to be razor-sharp. When the ball's at the other end for a long period I keep my concentration by walking out to the 18-yard line and continually adjusting my position as though attacks are coming from different directions. I might also do a few exercises.

DON'TS Avoid distractions, such as talking to the crowd behind your goal, team-mates or even the opposition. I've seen 'keepers chatted up by an opponent, lose concentration, and allow that same opponent to score!

SHOUTING

DO'S As you're in the privileged position of seeing all the play, use it to shout instructions to less well-placed team-mates. Act as a second pair of

Ray and Kevin Keegan pass on a few tips to a potential England 'keeper of the future.

eyes for them. Let them know what you're doing, and be boss in your patch.

DON'TS You might put off one of your defenders by shouting at him when he's got everything under control. Button your lip.

EMERGENCY!

DO'S Your defence is caught square up near the half-way line. The ball is lobbed over their heads and a forward has burst through in pursuit. You have two options. The first is to race out of your area and kick the ball clear. But you can only do this if the ball is closer to you than to him, and you have to make up your mind in a split-second.

The second option in this one-against-one situation is to spread yourself in front of him as large as possible to either delay him until a team-mate can put in a tackle, or block his shot with some part of your anatomy.

DON'TS If you can't realistically get the ball, then keep goalside — and keep cool.

FRANK McAVENNIE'S BEST FRIEND

FRANK McAVENNIE gave up football to watch Kenny Dalglish ... and then cried when he left Celtic for Liverpool.

"As a lad I preferred following Celtic and Kenny to playing," says West Ham's Scottish international goal-machine.

"When Kenny was transferred to Liverpool in 1977, I thought the end of the world had come. I just cried my eyes out. It was like losing a friend.

"I didn't dream that I would lined up alongside my boyhood idol when making my full debut for Scotland against Australia in the World Cup last year."

Sixteen League goals in his first four months with West Ham, following his summer move from St. Mirren had earned Frank his first cap ... and the roaring approval of 68,000 fanatical Hampden Park fans. Especially when he crowned an impressive performance with a brilliantly taken second-half goal.

Sensation

Young, handsome, well-groomed, friendly and enjoying a meteoric rise to fame, you'd think this striking sensation was very much a man about town. Well, you'd be wrong.

The bright lights of London hold no attraction for the 25-year-old Scot from Paisley.

"When I first came down from St. Mirren certain sections of the Press gave me a 'bad-boy' image. That was a load of rubbish.

"Sure I had been to a few discos in Glasgow and enjoyed the odd pint after a game. But that didn't mean I was a boozer or playboy.

"I suppose because Charlie Nicholas and Mo Johnston are both Scots, strikers and got themselves into bother that I'd do the same.

"I used to see Charlie regularly in Glasgow, but I've hardly spoken to him since coming South.

Surprise

"But I was determined not to do anything stupid. I had waited a long time to get a move from St. Mirren and wasn't going to do anything stupid and mess up my career."

Surprisingly it was George Best, a well-known hell-raiser in his time, who helped keep Frank on the straight and narrow.

"I got to know George through my agent Bill McMurdo, who acts for him as well. George had experienced the pitfalls of stardom and warned me to keep my nose clean."

From the start Frank decided to ensure he concentrated 100 per cent on his game and not outside interests. He moved into a West Ham club flat in the peace and quiet of Brentwood, Essex, with his girl friend, Anita.

"She made all the difference. London can be a lonely place as Charlie Nicholas found out. If you are on your own you are tempted to go out just for the company.

"I have since moved into a nice detached house in Hornchurch which is about 20 minutes from West Ham's training ground at Chadwell Heath.

"We only go to Upton Park on match days, so playing there is still special ... still a novelty.

"I love living in Essex. Who needs the West End? When you get there you can't find a place to park. So I don't bother."

Frank's spectacular baptism of fire in the English First Division attracted a great deal of media attention.

He appeared on ITV's "Saint and Greavesie' show on Saturday lunch-time. He was a guest of Terry Wogan.

But because of the soccer TV ban millions of fans missed the early exploits of this exciting goal-ace.

ITV reporter Martin Tyler took Frank on to busy Waterloo Bridge and asked passers-by if they could identify the First Division newcomer.

Without the benefit of the box only one could — famous Scottish comedian Billy Connolly.

"I've no intention of pushing myself into the glare of publicity," says Frank. "All I want is to score goals for West Ham and Scotland ... and win honours.

McAmany

"I've been called Frank McGinty, McVitie and McViney. But they can call me what they like."

Frank will apreciate one name some of the West Ham fans have invented for him ... McAmany.

It's incredible that Frank joined West Ham in the first place.

When West Ham boss John Lyall went to watch Frank for the first time he fractured his skull before half-time.

Fortunately, Lyall had seen enough in that Scottish Cup Quarter-Final tie against Dundee United to recognise potential and talent.

"Sign him but don't go a a penny over £100,000," was the advice John Lyall received from one famous First Division manager.

"Don't take a chance, he's a bit of a tearaway," warned another.

Lyall ignored the "advice" and paid

George at his Best for Manchester United at West Ham in 1972.

No hell-raiser —thanks to George

£340,000 for a player unknown outside Glasgow.

"I remember the papers at the time," says Frank. "Even though I had played for Scotland Under-21's they ran headlines — 'Frank Who?'.

"To make matters worse I was played out of position on my debut for the Hammers at Birmingham City, because the boss thought an attacking midfield role would take the pressure of goalscoring off me.

"But Paul Goddard was injured in that first game of the 1985-86 season. I moved up front and scored."

McAvennie's natural ability and fighting spirit made him an instant hit with the Upton Park faithful. Yet he wasn't always a feared figure.

"I was so skinny as a youngster I was usually stuck out on the wing out of harm's way."

Nicknamed "Bambi" because of his ungainly build, Frank left school at 16 and began a career with Glasgow City Corporation.

"I was handed a brush and shovel and told to sweep the streets. The job lasted 20 minutes."

McAvennie went on to lay tarmac, dig holes, wait on tables, and heave barrels around the White Horse Whisky distillery.

Painter

"I even worked as a mechanic, delivered bread and tried my hand at painting and decorating."

Then a couple of mates persuaded Frank to dust off his boots and play for a local amateur team. Eighteen months later he was at St. Mirren.

Frank stayed five years at Love Street hoping that one day a top English club would make an offer.

"West Ham's interest came right out of the blue," he recalls. "My boss at St. Mirren, Alex Miller and I had flown down to London to meet Luton manager David Pleat. But he wasn't at the hotel when we arrived.

"That didn't impress me too much. Nor did the terms offered by Mr. Pleat when he eventually turned up.

"We came out of the hotel jumped into a taxi and on to a meeting with John Lyall.

"It didn't take much persuading for me to know my future was at West Ham.

"John Lyall simply told me: 'I've seen you play. All I want is for you to go out and do the business.'"

Frank McAmany did that all right!

BEST of all time

BORN in Belfast in April, 1946 George Best is recognised as one of the greatest individual British players of all time.

Joined Manchester United at 17 when he made his First Division debut. Won the first of his 37 Northern Ireland caps shortly afterwards.

Scored 147 League goals in a sizzling United career which spanned ten years, reaching a peak in 1968 when he gained British and European Footballer of the Year awards and clinched a European Cup winners medal after United had won two Championships in 1965 and 1967.

Alex Ferguson.

Smashed the Old Firm

SINCE Alex Ferguson breezed into Pittodrie in 1978 there's never been a dull moment.

Aberdeen were looking for a big-name successor to Billy McNeill who had quit after just one year in charge to return to Celtic.

Fergie had been sensationally sacked by St. Mirren and was available. And when he was offered the opportunity to move North he didn't hesitate.

It's been success all the way for Fergie and his dandy Dons, who quickly won the Scottish Premier Division in 1979-80 to smash the Old Firm domination of Celtic and Rangers.

When Willie Miller collected the Skol Cup at Hampden in October, 1985, the trophy collection was complete.

But while his many Championship and Scottish Cup victories were moments to be cherished, Fergie will always recall the night of May 11, 1983, as his greatest achievement.

That's when Spanish giants Real Madrid were outfought and outclassed in Gothenburg and goals by Eric Black

and John Hewitt earned Aberdeen a 2-1 triumph in the European Cup Winners' Cup Final.

It was a victory that put Aberdeen firmly on the world soccer map — and made Fergie one of the most sought-after bosses in the game.

But when the big clubs were on his trail Fergie didn't want to know. Even when Rangers, the club he had supported and then played for, made him their number one choice to replace John Greig he steadfastly refused.

Not even the lure of the lira could tempt him from Pittodrie. When Inter Milan made a big-money move, a quick "arrivederci" from Fergie had their representative on his way back to Italy.

Why does he turn down such oppor-

A matter of fact

ABERDEEN'S original colours were black and gold. They switched to red and white in 1939.

THE Dons were founded in 1903 but had to wait unitl 1946 for their first major honour when they defeated Rangers 3-2 in the League Cup Final. And a year later they were celebrating again when Hibs were beaten 2-1 in the Scottish Cup Final. Their first Championship success was in 1955.

ALEX Ferguson is Aberdeen's eighth — and by far the most successful — manager since the War. The others were Dave Halliday, Dave Shaw, Tommy Pearson, Eddie Turnbull, Jimmy Bonthrone, Ally MacLeod and Billy McNeill. MacLeod quit in 1977 to become Scotland boss, a post taken up by Fergie in 1985.

JIM Leighton (right) is not the first Aberdeen goalkeeper to play for Scotland. But he has already won more caps than the other three — Fred Martin (6), Bobby Clark (17) and Ernie McGarr (2) — put together.

ABERDEEN'S record attendance is unlikely ever to be beaten. A crowd of 45,061 saw the Scottish Cup-tie

against Hearts in 1954 but in 1978 The Dons transformed Pittodrie into Britain's first all-seated stadium with a 23,000 capacity.

NOT only do Aberdeen have the country's smallest Board of Directors but all three of them — chairman Dick Donald, his son Ian and vice-chairman Chris Anderson — are former Pittodrie professionals. Ian Donald also had a brief spell with Manchester United.

tunities?

"That's an easy question to answer," he says. "I've already got a good job. Simple as that.

"There is still a great deal to achieve with Aberdeen and I'm very happy here. Job satisfaction counts for a lot."

That's bad news for the other clubs chasing honours ... but a real boost for Aberdeen and their fans who will never tire of Fergie's trophy-winning habit!

Skipper Willie Miller's confession

ABERDEEN have had their fair share of colourful characters at Pittodrie in the past but no one can match the achievements of captain Willie Miller (right).

For example, no Aberdeen skipper has ever collected more silverware. And Miller's way out in front as the club's most capped player.

Now an immaculate central defender, Miller actually arrived at Pittodrie in 1971 with ambitions to establish himself as a striker.

But he recalls: "It wasn't long before the club converted me into a defender. They had a few injury problems, I was asked to step in and I've been there ever since!"

GREAT SCOTT

ALEX Ferguson would be the first to admit that Teddy Scott is Mr Aberdeen.

Teddy first joined the club in 1954 as a promising centre-half and apart from a brief spell at Brechin towards the end of his playing career he's been with The Dons ever since.

No job is too big or to small for Teddy, one of the game's unsung heroes.

There's a nice story that sums up his value. The Dons were playing in Switzerland and while Teddy had packed the hamper he didn't make the trip.

Upon arrival it was discovered he'd put in the wrong colour shorts. "That's the sack for Scott when we get back," laughed Fergie.

Midfield star Gordon Strachan, now with Manchester United, quipped: "Well, that'll be ten jobs up for grabs!"

THE HIT

'Are we a dying breed?'

asks IAN RUSH

The box was packed with some of the hardest defenders in the world, the ball was at an impossible height and Mark Hughes was standing at the wrong angle. But with a devastating display of acrobatics, timing and sheer inspiration he scissor-volleyed one of the greatest goals I have ever seen.

We were linked together up front to break down Spain in a crucial World Cup-tie at Wrexham. I had nudged us in front, but Mark broke Spain's heart with that explosive second goal and we marched on to win 3-0.

Mark's goal — and one by me in Glasgow, a thundering volley from a Hughes inspired knock-down — were the products of professional strikers, consistent goalscorers ... HIT MEN.

Goals are the lifeblood of the game. How many players and managers have said that over the years? But it remains true, even more so in an era when the game is faster, the competitors fitter and the choking tactics so often designed to limit space and openings.

Most pros score a few goals during their careers — defenders pop up with set-piece headers or unexpected

Gary Lineker (below) can bullet head-ers from all angles. A different type of finisher to Andy Gray (right) and guaranteed to score twice as many goals.

MEN

one-off blasters from 35 yards; midfield players graft to produce between five and eight goals each in about 60 outings.

The likes of John Wark at Liverpool and Bryan Robson at Manchester United are exceptions. But we are the men who must top off all the brilliant work of our team-mates. We are the players who can get a minimum of touches in a game because of limpet-marking and yet must return a healthy goal-balance ... or face the sack.

Chelsea's Kerry Dixon impresses me. He has scored goals at every level, began his international career with four in two games for England and sustained a magnificent finishing rate, season after season.

Critics have bayed for his head when he has fluffed penalties or missed sitters. But he is usually the player who gets on the end of the ball inside the box and he is the man who steps up to take spot-kicks.

Critics have said Kerry would struggle in the Second Division when Chelsea signed him from Reading. They were wrong. They claimed he would find life tough in the First. They were wrong again. Kerry will always score.

He is not afraid to miss. Kerry is without doubt a professional hit-man.

Everton, our closest rivals, upset a few fans last year when they sold Andy Gray and replaced him with Leicester's Gary Lineker. But they did the right thing!

Andy is brave, strong and brilliant in the air and as a target man. He gets a reasonable haul of goals, averaging I'd say between 12 and 16 a season. He is also a god-send for lads who play alongside him because he creates so many great chances.

But Lineker is a hit-man. He has pace off the mark, instant control, shoots without massive backlift and can bullet headers from all angles. Over any season, at any level, I'd say Gary would score twice as many goals as Andy — they are very different players.

People make the mistake of singling out spectacular goals as the sign of a great finisher. Some players score great goals — others are great goal scorers. There is a massive difference!

Check back over the years and the same names will keep appearing … Jimmy Greaves, Roger Hunt, Gerd Muller, Denis Law, Allan Clarke, Malcolm Macdonald, Francis Lee, and Bob Latchford.

Some of those names will surprise you. But ignore reputations and check the figures — all those scored goals at whatever level they played and scored all kinds of goals.

You must get your regular fair share of the scruffy goals. I've knocked 'em over the line from a matter of inches, toe-poked, chested, kneed and even had one go in off my bum.

It's being there that matters — having the nose for the half chance, the rebound, the deflection. Don't ask me why I've stood in a certain place during a crazy goalmouth scramble. All I know is my instinct takes over and I'll take up a certain position in the box.

I've read Greaves and Macdonald make the same point. Goals were their trade-mark. It didn't matter that not all of them were picture-book net-breakers.

Back to the modern game — and you have to take off your hat to Frank McAvennie who came to West Ham from St. Mirren back in the summer of 1985, barely known and went on to poach goals of all types in a superb Football League baptism. Frank, even with a lean spell, is a hit-man.

At the other end of the age-scale I rate Peter Withe, so often described as a target man, a great bustling leader and superb with his head. But Peter is close to his 200th first class goal in a much-travelled career. He's scored at every level with incredible consistency. Yes, a hit-man.

First-rate finisher

Few players have received so much unfair stick as Watford's former England striker Luther Blissett. Yet you cannot argue with statistics — and they establish him as a first-rate finisher.

Luther has found the net consistently in all four divisions, blazed through great Cup exploits, rattled a hat-trick for England in his second appearance, and despite a disappointing season with AC Milan, you'll find he scored a few in Italy as well.

Celtic's Mo Johnston is an eye-catching young striker with pace and composure inside the box. He connects wth a high percentage of balls thrown into that most con-

Below: Master blaster Mark Hughes, one of the deadliest strikers in the world, has scored many spectacular goals… like this flying header against Aston Villa at Old Trafford. Right: Aberdeen's Eric Black makes a habit of hitting vital Cup goals.

gested of areas and his flair for goals earned him Scotland recognition ... which he promptly rewarded by scoring goals for his country.

And Aberdeen produced a gem in Eric Black who became something of an expert in Cup Finals, scoring in Cup Winners' Cup, Scottish Cup and League Cup Finals, won by The Dons.

One of Eric's deceptive talents is his heading ability. Not your traditional big aerial competitor, he has the Denis Law knack of appearing to hang for the extra few seconds and punch the ball with his forehead.

My biggest fear is that modern football, with so much at stake and so many levels of incredible fitness and pace being reached, will produce fewer hit-men as the years go by.

Too many youngsters brand themselves as midfield players — and I often wonder if this is because they are unsure where they should really play!

We end up with hundreds of lads prepared to run their legs off instead of finding their best positions and working at their strengths.

In fairness, fine players such as Ray Kennedy and Kenny Swain began as strikers and finished up winning their top honours in other roles — midfield and full-back respectively.

But I sometimes wish young lads would take the plunge a bit more and declare 'I'm a goalscorer, try me!'

More and more players will find scoring more simple by arriving late from deep positions, thus reducing the time during which they can be marked. This knack makes Wark and Robson deadly. I just hope we are still as deadly an element in the game when I'm back on the terraces, a retired hit-man with a hunger to see goals.

The 'Old Firm' derby games between Scottish giants Celtic and Rangers occasionally fail to reach dizzy heights in the skill-stakes. But they always create an atmosphere of great passion, commitment and 90 minutes of flat-out action. Here we see Davie McKinnon of Rangers (left) soaring above Paul McStay of Celtic in a typical clash. The Glasgow rivals have dominated their national games for decades. And while the likes of Aberdeen and Dundee United have emerged to lift major honours and enjoy spells of superiority, its the gutsy traditional fare of the 'Old Firm' duo that still packs grounds as no other Scottish fixture ever will.

The arguments raged for months before fans in London accepted that Chris Waddle is one of the best wingers in the modern game. Signed from Newcastle United in the summer of 1985, he came to multi-million pound Spurs in a blaze of publicity as Peter Shreeve paraded what he really believed was a Championship-winning squad. Sadly he reckoned without his occasionally woeful defence — and his incorrect selection of Waddle in a free-roaming role. But once the Geordie got back on his favourite flank, his crosses, direct running and goalscoring brought the fans out of their expensive White Hart Lane seats. Despite a few spluttering displays, he also had an almighty hand in England's 1986 World Cup qualification, repaying manager Bobby Robson's faith in his skills with some splendid solo moments and an international scoring breakthrough. Waddle — badly missed by United — is now one of London's hottest properties.

CRASH, BANG, WADDLE!

FOOTBALL LEAGUE
CUP FINAL
1969
Arsenal 1, Swindon Town 3
By Bob Wilson

Cup ... until Bobby Gould followed up a half-chance to head us level.

"I'll never forget how much we celebrated that moment, leaping off towards our fans, arms aloft, close to tears with relief — but if we thought Swindon were broken, we were wrong.

"Don Rogers chose extra-time to etch his name into folklore with a snappy shot to put them back in front and a tremendous

'Wembley shocker'

"I'll never forget my first Wembley Final with Arsenal because the result shook football to its roots.

"No disrespect to Swindon Town but Arsenal had lost the previous Final 1-0 to Leeds, had a powerful line-up, albeit weakened by illness to some players beforehand and were definite favourites.

"Wembley was a disgrace, the pitch a bumpy, muddy mess. But that is not why we were beaten because Town had to play on it as well — and they played extremely well.

"Roger Smart cashed in on a dreadful defensive mix-up to give Swindon the lead. We battled and pounded away at their goal without success and it looked as if that goal would win them the

solo burst that ended with him sweeping round me to plonk the third in our net.

"I often think back on that amazing day — and shudder."

Arsenal are left for dead as Don Rogers (not in photo) puts Swindon ahead.

74

'THERE'

'Humiliation'

"The worst night of my footballing life is the only way to sum up this humiliation. We were into a terrible run of 16 games without a win, sliding towards the foot of the First Division and in dire need of a good Cup run to lift hopes and the fans.

"Gola League Altrincham, though a good side, should never have been in with a shout. It showed our level of confidence when I admit that we did not relish the game from the start.

"But we buckled down, overcame our nerves and I actually fired us into the lead after 64 minutes. I felt such a flood of relief because it was my first goal in five months — yes, it was that kind of period at St. Andrews.

"But before we could turn the screw, Altrincham rocked us with an equaliser through a mass of legs in the box — and I sensed our nerves surfacing. So did our worried fans.

"Imagine how I felt, therefore, when my woeful backpass in extra time was rolled too far wide of David Seaman and trickled over the line for their winner! I was a City fan as a kid and a fanatic for the cause as a player. Yet I'd made our season doubly bad. I went home, slammed the door and opened a bottle.

"Manager Ron Saunders resigned a few days later because his correct appeal for money to strengthen the squad was again turned down. It was all a living nightmare!"

Non-League Altrincham celebrate a major F.A. Cup upset at St. Andrews.

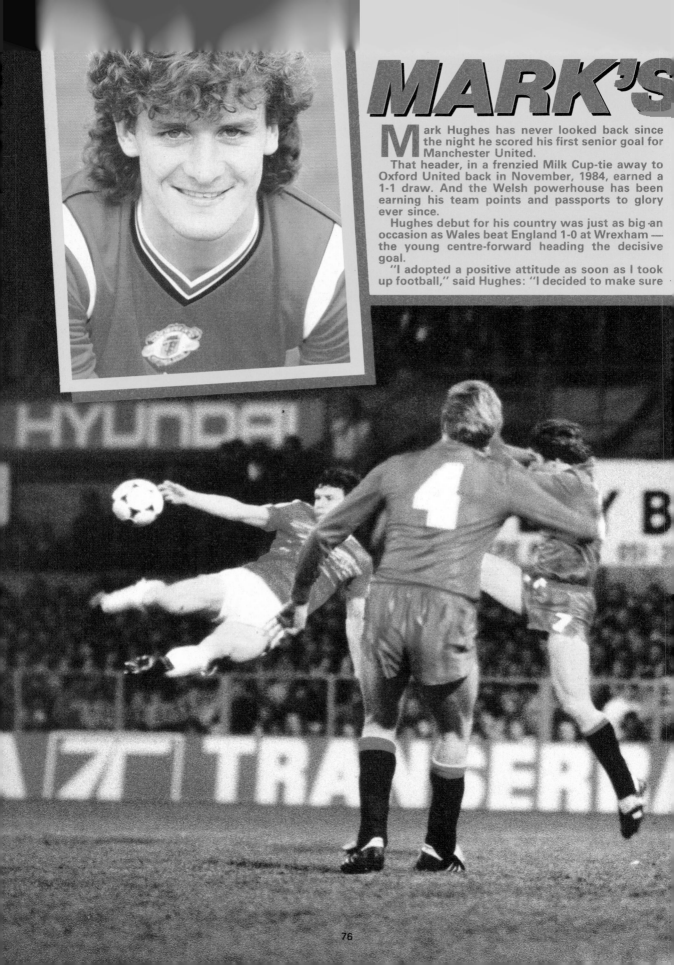

MARK'S

Mark Hughes has never looked back since the night he scored his first senior goal for Manchester United.

That header, in a frenzied Milk Cup-tie away to Oxford United back in November, 1984, earned a 1-1 draw. And the Welsh powerhouse has been earning his team points and passports to glory ever since.

Hughes debut for his country was just as big an occasion as Wales beat England 1-0 at Wrexham — the young centre-forward heading the decisive goal.

"I adopted a positive attitude as soon as I took up football," said Hughes: "I decided to make sure

MAGIC GOALS!

I was able to look after myself physically and once I had that confidence I knew the ability would show.

"I have been criticised for my aggressive style. But this is a game for men, a physical game in which you give and take knocks in the chase for honours.

"I don't score enough of the scruffy goals, the tap ins and close-range stabs that add up to 30 goals a season.

"My mate and Welsh partner Ian Rush has the nose for those goals as well as the spectacular shots and powerful headers. We complement each other at international level.

"But I spend more time outside the box, as a target man and going deep to collect the ball. I am certain I'll home in on more of the bread and butter goals as my career develops. But for the time being I'm determined to sustain the start I have made. That means getting the better of the best defenders in the League.

"I have special goals I remember — like the scissors-kick special (below) I pulled off against Spain in a World Cup game in 1985. It was too low to head and too high to kick, but somehow I managed to contort my body to connect.

"My favourite? I'll never forget my winner against Liverpool in the 1985 FA Cup Semi-Final replay. Now that was a strike to savour."

The Commandos

Football's all-action men

WHEN Ron Saunders asked Chris Nicholl to sell him Joe Jordan, the West Bromwich Albion manager was seeking a special type of player to lead his skilful but punchless First Division stragglers.

The fact that Jordan is 34 meant nothing to Saunders, or that the former Scotland international striker rarely tops 15 goals a season.

Jordan is, in a football sense, one of the game's 'Commandos' — strong, brave, ruthless, a winner and a natural leader — in his case of his forward line.

Every team needs one, great sides are built round them, winning outfits respond to them when their form is dipping and they are miles from home.

The best known Commando in

Europe these days is a curly-haired Scot with velvet touch inside chain-mail armour. Graeme Souness of Sampdoria and Scotland is one of the best captains in the world.

"I have never deliberately hurt another player in my life," he says: "but football is a game for men, a competitive, physical contest where the stongest as well as the most talented come out on top. I will never shirk a challenge, duck a tackle or shy away from responsibility."

Souness can shred a defence with one glorious ball ... and do the same to an opponent rash enough to attempt rough stuff or sly digs.

Above all, he organises, inspires and leads with his back straight, his head up and his stare fixed.

All the truly successful teams of the past have boasted such a man

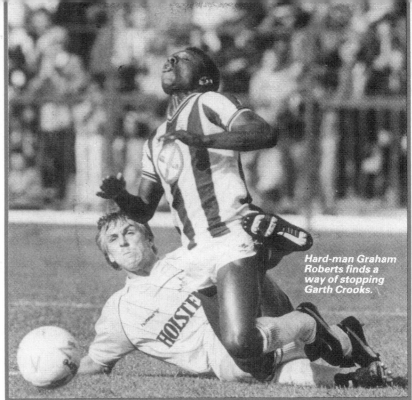

Hard-man Graham Roberts finds a way of stopping Garth Crooks.

Graeme Souness has never shirked a challenge.

— Dave Mackay of Spurs, Tommy Smith of Liverpool, Billy Bremner of Leeds, Bobby Murdoch of Celtic, John Greig of Rangers and Peter Storey at Arsenal.

Today we have a new breed. But they share an age-old quality — courage. "I cannot change my style, although I know it will lead to a certain amount of injury problems," admits Manchester United and England captain Bryan Robson.

"I advised our defender Kevin Moran how to use his arms as a protective shield when going for high balls — perfectly fair and necessary for a player of his guts and determination. It cut down his facial injuries. Yet I cannot stop myself from going in for tackles that will sometimes risk an almighty whack."

Robson allies this forceful, brave style to pace and skill and emerges a Commando of the S.A.S. variety.

Celtic's Roy Aitken suffered the humiliation of being sent off in the 1984 Scottish Cup Final against Aberdeen, for a bulldozing tackle, the first player to be dismissed in the Final since 1929. But he overcame the memory to play a major role in his team's triumph in the 1985 Final against Dundee United.

"It was an awful moment," says Aitken: "But I had to take my punishment, put the whole thing out of my mind and get on with my game. It never entered my head in the next Final."

Aitken's game is compulsive viewing — all strength, courage, driving ambition and versatility. In defence or midfield, for club or country, Aitken never hides, always supports men on the ball, wins it like a terrier and uses it positively. A player you always want on your side and never as an opponent.

When multi-million pound Spurs start to wobble round their cheque stubs, they send for former Weymouth part-timer Graham Roberts, whose whole attitude to the modern game has elevated him from non-League football to international stardom.

Everton's long-overdue dominance on Merseyside was greatly assisted by the presence of Peter Reid in midfield. The former Bolton Wanderers player overcame a frightening list of serious injuries to star in a splendid League Championship, FA Cup winning and Cup Winners' Cup winning team.

Reid, whose excellent form took him into the England team, is a master-tackler and a man who can hold a team together when the seas get choppy then lead them onto the offensive by making them play.

"Yes, I can tackle well," he says: "But I get tired of being described as a tackler first and foremost. I can also control a ball, beat opponents and pass!"

Peter Reid, like many excellent British players, is a real, all-action Commando!

Dependable Dave rocked Brazil

Dundee United's rock-solid central defender Dave Narey has earned himself the tag 'Mr Dependable'.

In 13 years at Tannadice he has missed only a handful of games and in helping United to the forefront of both the domestic and European scenes he has taken his appearance total beyond the 500 mark.

Narey, born in Dundee 30 years ago, was one of manager Jim McLean's first signings. At that time he was still at school but the pair have since come a long way together.

United were not one of the country's more fashionable outfits when Narey was first called up. But along with skipper Paul Hegarty he has been the cornerstone of the most successful side in the club's history.

The trophy cabinet at his Tayside home is packed wth souvenirs that tell their own story. He was ever-present, significantly, when United landed their very first title in 1983 and he played a leading role in the 1980 and 1981 League Cup triumphs.

At international level, too, Narey had enjoyed considerable success. After winning youth and Under-21 honours he made the first of many senior appearances in a friendly against Sweden at Hampden in 1977 when he helped Scotland to a 3-1 win.

First cap

"Winning my first senior cap was a tremendous thrill," he recalls, "and the fact that I was the first player from Dundee United ever to play for my country was the icing on the cake.

"But the memory I treasure more than any other as a Scotland player has to be my goal against Brazil in the World Cup Finals in Spain four years ago."

Manager Jock Stein drafted him in at right-back against the men from Brazil to counter the huge threat posed by their talented left-winger Eder.

The move paid off handsomely, if unexpectedly, after only 18 minutes when Narey rounded off a nine-man movement to thunder a tremendous volley beyond the stunned Brazilian goakeeper Waldir Peres.

That Brazil equalised through Zico 15 minutes later and scored three more without reply did nothing to detract from Narey's moment of glory.

Yet the modest six-footer had no idea his career would reach such a fabulous peak when it got off to a distinctly low-key start back in 1973.

He explains: "My debut was against Falkirk at Tannadice on a Wednesday afternoon. It was a re-arranged game that had originally been abandoned because of fog.

"It was during a miners' strike, floodlit football was banned and therefore a crowd of just over 1,000 turned up. I'm told there hasn't been a lower attendance at Tannadice since the War so I never have any bother remembering my first appearance."

'CONCORDE'

Mark Hateley the prototype for the shape of today's slim-line striker.

HIGH-FLIERS TAKE-OFF

This is the age of jet-propelled strikers. Men built like thoroughbred racehorses with the speed and stamina to match.

Gone are the days when an international centre-forward needed to be built the size of a Jumbo jet with rippling 'Rambo' muscles beneath his shirt.

Today's striker is as slim as Concorde and gives a supersonic performance to match Britain's greatest commercial aircraft.

The 1986 World Cup tournament in Mexico marked the arrival of a new super-breed of goal-poacher.

They looked hungry, they looked lean and sharp, and they looked mean!

But bruising warhorses like Everton's England striker Dixie Dean would take one look at today's slim-line goal-machine from Wales, Ian Rush, and think the game had gone soft.

In Dixie's day many a fresh-faced youngster was turned away from League clubs because 'you're too small to make a footballer, lad'. Heartbreaking for the kids with ambitions to make the top but illustrative of times when lightweights with the number nine shirt on their backs were as rare as television sets.

England's World Cup striker Mark Hateley's physique illustrates the prototype for the new shape of star international bosses are employing these days.

Stealth, cunning and burning speed is the rule. You don't get giants, however light on their feet, showing the deftness of touch to smash down modern defences.

Hateley's 6ft 1in frame, pressed neatly into the Coventry, Portsmouth, AC Milan and England shirts he has worn with pride these last few years, pushes the weighing scales to just 11 stone 7 lbs, and a lot less than that at times in the fierce heat of Mexico last summer.

Ian Rush, who became one of Europe's most lethal marksmen at Liverpool, stands an inch taller than Hateley and weighs 12 stone 6 lbs, which represents only a few more pounds than little 5ft 7ins Francis Lee scaled in the days he scored goals with regularity for Manchester City and England.

Continued over

Paul Walsh is impossible to mark when he's on top form.

Managers have been encouraged to turn to the mean and hungry type of striker to meet the demands of the world game.

As defenders become fitter and sharper, so strikers have been forced to match them for mobility.

Today's striker is expected to slog for hours in training to lose vital pounds. Only the nimblest striker stands a chance of outmanoeuvring the sleek defenders that dominate the world game today.

England's change in style has been coming since Ron Greenwood tried to find a successful attacking force for the 1982 World Cup Finals.

The England boss resisted fierce pressure from the media to launch West Bromwich Albion's burly 13 stone favourite Cyrille Regis on the French and the Czechs in Bilbao.

Greenwood preferred quicksilver strikers like Trevor Francis, Tony Woodcock and Kevin Keegan.

It is true that he took Ipswich Town's Paul Mariner to Spain. At six foot tall and weighing 12 stone 6 lbs, Mariner was a formidable specimen and had the mobility and the goal-scoring record for England to keep his place.

Greenwood had never enjoyed the same success when employing big Bob Latchford. Everton's burly striker had a phenomenal League scoring record but his five England goals in a dozen appearances never matched his club performances.

Yet successive England managers before Greenwood helped pioneer the new era of lean strikers leant heavily on the juggernaut type attackers in their search for success.

Warhorse

The big Bolton Wanderers favourite Nat Lofthouse, Busby Babe Tommy Taylor, old West Brom warhorse Derek Kevan, Spurs' double winning champion Bobby Smith, World Cup winning hero Geoff Hurst, Everton's Joe Royle and Martin Chivers, another Tottenham favourite, were all from the school of battering-ram giants, renowned for their muscular, no-nonsense approach rather than the sublime goal-scoring skills of a Rossi, Platini or Rush.

Their approach was essential to the needs of those times. Who will forget Geoff Hurst hurling his 13 stone frame against the might of the West German defence in scoring a World Cup winning hat-trick for England in 1966?

No one complained he was too big in those days. But would the former West Ham favourite have enjoyed so much freedom to manoeuvre his large frame through today's air-tight rearguards?

West Ham's John Lyall clearly has no reservations about his current goal-scoring phenomenon, Tony Cottee, who scales 11 stone at 5ft 8ins. Cottee's secret? Size means nothing. He's simply as quick as Rush in the penalty-area, snatching goals that leaden-footed, more ponderous strikers would never sniff.

No one is seeking to denigrate the records of Britain's international 'giants' of the past, simply to point out that their style in the immediate post-War era would not always work today.

Who, for instance, can complain about Nat Lofthouse's contribution to England's re-building operation after the last War.

The big Bolton Wanderers

centre-forward never let England down with his no-nonsense tactics in the 1950's, scoring 30 international goals in 33 England appearances.

Tottenham's burly Bobby Smith, a member of their double winning team, averaged almost a goal a game in 15 England appearances.

He formed a thrilling attacking partnership with the prolific goal-scoring imp Jimmy Greaves which saw Smith's brawn taking the weight off his sharp-shooting sidekick for Greavsie to flourish in the spaces created.

One football record book described Smith as 'overweight and sluggish' when he left Chelsea for Spurs in an £18,000 transfer deal in 1955. It goes on to record that at Spurs Smith as 'transformed into a slimline, bustling, brave goal grabber of the highest order, scoring 28 League goals in the fabulous double winning season'.

as he had First Division rearguards.

The England manager clearly preferred the more mobile style of Gary Lineker alongside Hateley.

Lineker, weighing only 11 stone 10 lbs, is as sharp and as pacey as a runaway stag, just the talents necessary these days.

Splash out

Liverpool striker Paul Walsh weighs even less, just 10 stone 8 lbs. He is impossible to mark when he touches the form that persuaded Liverpool to splash out £750,000 to transfer him from Luton in 1984.

Critics of this argument will complain that there are times when sheer physical presence is essential to break down modern defences.

They suggest that there are times when big, burly players

hurling themselves onto the end of free kicks is worth twice as much as the dainty stuff.

That point is countered by managers who employ the services of defenders in an attacking role at set-pieces. Terry Butcher, the England centre-half, has earned a frightening reputation for scoring goals, and Everton's centre-half Derek Mountfield embarrassed many a striker in the 1984-85 season when his 12 stone 7 lbs frame smashed down First Division defences to reap a personal haul of 10 goals in Everton's Championship winning season.

Who did they have up front? Two highly mobile 11 stoners, Andy Gray at 5ft 11ins and the 6ft 1in Graeme Sharp.

World Cup hero Geoff Hurst. But would he be a hit against modern defences?

Tony Cottee has proved size means nothing when you have the goal-touch.

Joe Royle and Martin Chivers, both 6ft 1in tall, carried on the tradition of 'Dreadnought' sized strikers into the Sixties and Seventies.

They all weighed 12 stone or over, essential bone covering to survive in those times of titanic collisions before referees tightened-up.

Only Kerry Dixon, of England's current crop of strikers, carries the weight of the old guard.

The Chelsea striker's brilliant goal-scoring record forced the England door open but Bobby Robson clearly needed some convincing that the 13 stone giant had the right style to crack foreign defences as successfully

Comparison Chart

		Height	Weight
PAST:	Martin Chivers Spurs and England	6.1	12.12½
PRESENT:	Mark Hateley AC Milan and England	6.1	11.7
PAST:	Geoff Hurst West Ham and England	5.11	12.9
PRESENT:	Trevor Francis England	5.11	11.7
PAST:	Francis Lee Man City and England	5.7	12.2
PRESENT:	Paul Walsh , Liverpool and England	5.7	10.8

THE BOSS

Kenny Dalglish (Liverpool), Mick Mills (Stoke City) and Frank Worthington (Tranmere Rovers) each have one thing in common — they are player-managers. So what problems are they facing? We put the question to some of those who have been through the mill, who know what it's like suddenly to change from shop-floor to management.

Kenny Dalglish copes with both jobs at Liverpool.

Suspicion
JOHN WILE
(Player-manager at Peterborough United)

You soon realise you have to be apart from your players.

I remember hearing Bobby Robson talking on the topic, and he put it in a nutshell when he said: "You've got to sit on another part of the bench."

You must have a rapport with your players, of course, but you've also got to have that distance between you.

In some respects that will start happening automatically, because players have a natural suspicion of you once you become boss. It's an in-built thing.

Player's respect
DENIS SMITH   (Manager York City)

At Kenny's level it is a totally different ball game to that facing Frank Worthington which is the one at which I started.

He'll have a lot more things to think about than just playing. Yet he's playing in the First Division and you have to give 100 per cent dedication to your playing because you're performing at the highest level in the world.

As long as you've got the respect of the players, you should have no major problems. Then it is just a matter of finding the time to do training.

Obviously when you become player-manager you're heading towards the end of your playing days, and that is when you need as much training as you can get!

You can find yourself having to be involved in business lunches and PR exercises. They are an inevitable part of the job but, of course, they can hinder your playing.

MEN

Bradford City's team behind the team. Terry Yorath (left) and Trevor Cherry.

Mind boggling
TREVOR CHERRY
(Player-manager at Bradford City)

As player-manager it is easy to try and do too much at the beginning. The organising and administration can leave you short for playing.

You also discover when you have a busy week in the office that it can affect your performance.

I remember approaching a game against York after a week in which one problem had crowded upon another. So by the time I came to put on my strip in the dressing room I recall thinking to myself 'What's next on the agenda?'

My mind was in a daze. It didn't register that it was a football match!

24 hour day
ALAN BALL
(ex-player-manager at Blackpool, now Portsmouth manager)

The difficulties include divorcing yourself from your particular performance each Saturday.

When you go onto the pitch as player-manager you are out there to play but in doing that you tend to forget your managerial role.

It is a thin dividing line between concentrating on your own play *and* thinking about the performances of others.

Then during the week you have to train to keep yourself fit and often coach at the same time which is not easy. There is also the paper work!

There are 24 hours in a day — and you've got to work most of them!

(Player-manager at Bristol City)

A good number two

A good assistant manager is vital to a player-manager.

You need somebody to share some of the pressure. He must be someone you trust completely and have the same ideas on how the game should be played.

So, if you're away on board meetings or tribunals, you know things will run smoothly.

I would also stress that you should not be afraid to make mistakes because you will do — almost every day! But that's how you learn.

TERRY COOPER

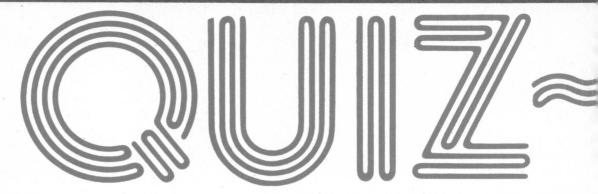

QUIZ~

1. Who said 'Football isn't a matter of life and death. It's more serious than that'?

2. Arsenal paid £1m for him, yet he never played a League game for them before being transferred to Crystal Palace. Can you name him?

3. Edson Arantes do Nascimento is the full name of a legendary Brazilian star. Who?

4. Which famous Liverpool player of The Seventies was nicknamed 'Little Mouse'?

5. The club is based in England, yet plays in the Scottish League. Got it?

6. Only two countries have achieved a hat-trick of World Cup wins each. Know them?

7. Who play soccer at Rugby Park?

8. Brian Clough enjoyed only a short reign at Elland Road as manager of Leeds United. How many days did it last?

9. How many Scotsmen played in Liverpool's 1977 European Cup win in Rome?

10. Who scored for both sides in the 1946 F.A. Cup Final, when Derby County beat Charlton 4-1 at Wembley?

You've probably played that popular indoor game Trivial Pursuit. Here we present a brain-teasing selection of questions about the amazing, the

11. Jimmy Greaves, the TV personality, once had a spell with an Italian club. Which one?

12. True or False? Two Third Division clubs have won the League Cup.

13. Which is the elder brother: John or Justin Fashanu?

14. Which manager of a British country has the surname of a rival home country?

15. Has the 100th Scottish Cup Final been played yet?

16. Everton have won a trophy that neighbours Liverpool have yet to capture. What is it?

17. Name the Arsenal star who was educated at a public school?

Q. 10

Q. 22

Q. 11

Q. 13

CHASE

unusual, the off-beat in the world of football. See how many you can answer off the top of your head in double-quick time. Ready, steady, go!

18. The Maracana, the World's largest ground, situated in Rio de Janeiro, Brazil, can hold how many fans?

19. What have Blackburn Rovers, Portsmouth, Preston, Burnley, Manchester City, Tottenham Hotspur, Leeds United and Derby County in common when it comes to Football League honours?

20. In season 1983-84 which Sheffield club set up an unbeaten run of 15 games in the Second Division?

21. Sir Alf Ramsey is the only manager to have won the Championships of the First, Second, and Third Divisions. Can you name the club he steered to this unique hat-trick?

22. Pat Jennings, the great Northern Ireland 'keeper with a record number of caps for his country, first played for which League club?

23. Who is the oldest player to turn out in First Division football? Clues: It was for Stoke City v Fulham in February, 1965; he was 50 years and 5 days old; and he was later knighted.

24. In 1983-84 who became the first British winner of the European Adidas Golden boot award with a total of 32 goals?

25. Name the striker whose individual trademark after scoring a goal is to celebrate by whirling his right arm like a windmill?

26. Celtic's most-capped player is a full-back. His name is — —?

27. Pop-loving Chelsea idol, 5'6" Pat Nevin, was once turned down by Celtic. Can you guess why?

28. 'Thames Ironworks' was once the name of which London club?

29. Nottingham Forest's Dutch midfield man Johnny Metgod previously played for which Spanish side?

30. Before joining Watford, John McClelland captained Glasgow Rangers. Which country has he won caps for — and it's not Scotland.

Answers on page 125.

Q. 27

Q. 29

Q. 30

SHOCK

Before Swindon's shock Milk Cup victory over Sunderland last season, LOU MACARI took his squad to an Army barracks for three days.

"The lads had to sleep on hard bunk beds and they did complain a little about having to take cold showers, but the food and practice facilities were excellent and the Army were very hospitable," asserts Macari.

We asked other managers to recall tough or unusual training schedules.

Sheffield Wednesday HOWARD WILKINSON, whose squad must rank among the fittest in the League, regards football as an endurance activity.

"Our weekly running sessions, which often take place around country hillsides and range from short sprints to one-and-a-half hour runs, are extremely demanding, but by varying times and locations, I think we manage to take the boredom out of it.

"In any case, running shouldn't be seen as a drudgery but as a way of improving you as a player," insists Wilkinson.

Coventry manager DON MACKAY, remembers a particularly arduous session from his Dundee days.

"I'd organised our annual pre-season cross-country run in the Highland woods and hills and,

Right: Howard Wilkinson's training routines have made Sheffield Wednesday one of the fittest teams in Britain.
Below: Jock Wallace organises his Rangers squad before taking them to the dreaded Gullane Sands.

TACTICS

For some clubs training is like a Commando assault course.

Left: Alan Ball is a 'big softie' at heart.
Above: Dave Bassett's methods at Wimbledon involve a great deal of ball work.

because I like to keep fit myself, I led the lads off.

"Three young apprentices decided that I wouldn't notice if they slipped off and took a short cut. But I did.

"I waited over an hour for them while the team coach went back to Dundee and eventually three lonely, mud-spattered bodies turned up, having run 14 miles more than their colleagues because they'd got lost.

"The next year they kept up with me all the way," adds Mackay with a chuckle.

Wimbledon, like Sheffield Wednesday, are renowned for their physical attributes, but manager DAVE BASSETT's most demanding routine does not only involve running.

"To help the players improve their ball-control and their stamina at the same time, we play a man-for-man game of six-or-seven-a-side, often on a full-size pitch," explains Bassett.

"This gives them practice at both marking and losing their marker, but it can only work in three-minute spells because the exercise is extremely strenuous.

"In fact, the whole session only lasts 20 minutes, but by the end, the lads have really earned a break, I can tell you," says Bassett firmly.

Although he was Mr Energy during his playing days, Portsmouth's ALAN BALL doesn't like giving his squad a hard time.

"I give them a tough run in the morning, which doesn't always go down too well, but our training sessions are generally low-key affairs. I'm a big softie, you see," reveals Ball.

"If we play badly, I don't drag the players through any gruelling routine as a punishment, either. I do all my ranting and raving when they're on the field."

The legendary disciplinarian, JOCK WALLACE of Rangers, has his own special recipe for sorting out the men from the boys before the start of a season. He takes his players to Gullane Sands, just outside Edinburgh, for a training routine that resembles a Commando assault course.

"The idea is to concentrate purely on stamina sprints and those energy-sapping sand dunes, all of which are at an angle of 75 degrees, are perfect," says Wallace.

"Every player has to complete 20 to 24 of these sprints and nobody is allowed to fail if they want to play for Rangers.

"I don't care if they have to crawl up those dunes on their hands and knees," barks the man who once told a young player who stopped to be sick during one such session: 'Hey son, if you're going to be sick, do it as you're running'!

GAME FOR A LAUGH

Ref: Name, son?
Strachan: It's ... er ... wait a moment ... it's on the tip of my tongue.

"Don't tell me the all-conquering, unbeatable invincibles have gone and got themselves knocked out of the Cup."

"Before we take this bounce-up will a certain gentleman lower his right boot."

Full-back's Excuse Me: Defenders Ray Ranson of Birmingham (left) and Kenny Sansom (Arsenal) join hands for a touchline waltz.

"Quick — red alert. Get the stretcher and smelling salts ready."

THE glare of publicity shone brightly on Hibs' fleet-footed marksman Gordon Durie last season.

Hardly a week went by without a big-name club being linked with the youngster. Spurs, Manchester United, Chelsea and Liverpool were among the many outfits to practically purchase season tickets for Easter Road.

Working quietly in the shadows, though, was Steve Cowan, rejected at Aberdeen by Alex Ferguson and bought for a bargain £50,000 by Hibs boss John Blackley.

And, in a fascinating tug-of-war on the goalscoring front, Durie and Cowan, team-mates in green-and-white, were rivals in the hit parade.

Stevie Wonder and Jukebox Durie — fashionably nicknamed by their adoring fans — climbed the charts at a scintillating rate bringing a smile to Blackley's face and scowls to rival defenders.

Cowan overcame injury problems to give his career the kiss of life. In true Roy of the Rovers fashion he resurrected his career. One minute he was heading for the scrapheap, the next he was shooting for stardom.

"Leaving Aberdeen was a tough decision," says Steve, "but it really turned out well for me.

"I wasn't sure of a first team game at Pittodrie such was the depth of the playing squad. There seemed to be about three players for every position.

"As any striker will tell you, confidence is everything. And to

STEVIE WONDER

gain that much-needed commodity you need a run of games in the top side.

"But, such was the pressure at Aberdeen, changes were made when the goods weren't instantly delivered.

"When I got the opportunity to go to Hibs I didn't hesitate. When I met manager John Blackley it took me about two minutes to get my signature on those transfer forms.

"I haven't looked back since. I thoroughly enjoyed my first year at Easter Road and I'm looking forward to the future."

Fair-haired Cowan dovetailed perfectly with Durie in their first season together.

"It was quite amazing," says Cowan. "You would have thought we were playing alongside each other all our lives.

"But he's an easy guy to team up with. His speed is quite startling. Sometimes he's too quick for his own good!

"However, he is totally unselfish. Most goalscorers tend to be a bit greedy, but although Gordon gets more than his share, he's not selfish.

"I think we've been good for each other."

Ironically, Cowan's first Cup Final for Hibs was against his old club Aberdeen in the League Cup at Hampden last season.

"Well, I certainly found out what it was like to play against my old mates that day," says Cowan. "They scored two early goals, then closed the game down.

"They're an immensely professional outfit and I can see Hibs are heading in the same direction."

GOAL!

OR WAS

He can't miss from there, or perhaps the 'keeper saved it? Did the ball hit the post or maybe a defender cleared the danger?

Study the pictures taken during last season's action and make up your mind. Was it a goal or not? Answers on page 125.

3

1

2

4

92

T?

1. Glenn Hoddle weaves his way round the Oxford defence and chips the ball over the advancing 'keeper Steve Hardwick during Tottenham's 5-1 victory at White Hart Lane.

2. With just Gary Bailey to beat, Chelsea's Joe McLaughlin powers in a header during their 2-1 defeat by Manchester United at Stamford Bridge.

3. Everton 'keeper Neville Southall looks dejected as Tony Cottee powers in during West Ham's 2-1 victory at Upton Park. But did Tony score?

4. Nottingham Forest midfielder Brian Rice's shot is virtually over the line as defender Russell Osman makes a desperate attempt to clear in Leicester's 3-0 defeat.

5. Panic in the Aberdeen defence as Celtic's Peter Grant forces his way through for a shot at goal in their 1-1 draw.

6. Sheffield Wednesday striker Lee Chapman heads the ball firmly past Newcastle 'keeper Martin Thomas in the 2-2 draw at Hillsboro.

EVERTON'S

Peter Reid with the 1985 Championship trophy.

Howard Kendall's £2 million winning team

Everton manager Howard Kendall has emerged as one of the shrewdest operators in the transfer market in recent years.

In his first five years in charge at Goodison Park, Kendall spent £5,265,000 on 26 players but recouped £3,171,000 of that by selling 30.

And while the Everton boss has occasionally broken the bank to sign men like Adrian Heath and Gary Lineker, it's Kendall's eye for a bargain which has made him such a successful manipulator of the market.

Peter Reid, Derek Mountfield, Neville Southall and Trevor Steven were all virtually unheard of in First Division circles when Kendall brought them to Goodison.

Now he's hoping to have the same success with young reserves such as Paul Wilkinson, Bobby Mimms, Darrin Coyle and Warren Aspinall.

Neville Southall

Position: Goalkeeper.
Joined Everton: July, 1981, £150,000 from Bury.
Analysis: Kendall's second signing for the club and arguably his best. Unable to hold down a regular place at first due to the dependability of Jim Arnold and even went to Port Vale on loan in January 1983. Established himself at the start of the 1984-85 season and has never looked back. Undisputed Welsh number one, his excellent reflexes deservedly won him the Footballer of the Year award for 1984-85.

Pat Van den Hauwe

Position: Left-back.
Joined Everton: September, 1984, £100,000 from Birmingham.
Analysis: Regarded as just another run of the mill First Division player before Kendall gave him the chance to prove his true worth in a class team. Quick, reliable and aggressive, England wanted him as cover for Kenny Sansom but Belgium-born Pat preferred to play for Wales. Proved his versatility by deputising brilliantly for the injured Mountfield in 1985-86.

Derek Mountfield

Position: Centre-half.
Joined Everton: June 1982, £30,000 from Tranmere.
Analysis: Mike Walsh, Glenn Keeley and Billy Wright had all failed to impress Kendall, but Mountfield struck up an immediate understanding with Kevin Ratcliffe when injury struck down Mark Higgins. Took to the First Division superbly and was outstanding during 1984-85, scoring 14 goals as a bonus. Sorely missed when ruled out the following season by a knee injury.

Paul Bracewell

Position: Centre midfield.
Joined Everton: May, 1984, £250,000 from Sunderland.
Analysis: A tireless but unspectacular worker, Bracewell's successful combination with Peter Reid was the key to Everton's incredible success in 1985. Showed much potential at an early age but seemed to have lost his way at Sunderland following a transfer from Stoke. Kendall used all the build-up to the 1984 F.A. Cup Final as a smokescreen to make his move and got his man on the eve of the big game. Won his first England cap in the summer of 1985.

GOLDEN BUYS

Trevor Steven

Position: Right midfield.
Joined Everton: July 1983, £300,000 from Burnley.
Analysis: Stood out as a potential diamond in a struggling Burnley team and Kendall had to beat off a number of challengers to get his man. But Steven's early performances for Everton were none too impressive and it looked as though he was going to become another Goodison miss. Returned to the team as less of a winger and more of a midfield player and the transformation was incredible. Came of age during the 1984 F.A. Cup Final when he tore Watford's defence apart. Scored 16 times the following season, and this eye for goal coupled with lightning acceleration soon earned him England recognition.

Peter Reid

Position: Centre midfield.
Joined Everton: December 1982, £60,000 from Bolton.
Analysis: Arsenal, Wolves and Everton had all been prepared to pay more than £400,000 for the England Under-21 international before a series of terrible injuries threatened to curtail the career of Reid. Kendall eventually got his man for a knockdown £60,000 and once Reid gained a regular place in the Everton midfield it soon became apparent why he had been so highly rated. A brilliant tackler and steadying influence on the youngsters around him, Reid's defensive covering enabled his more attacking team-mates the freedom to blast Everton to unparalleled success in '85. A tremendous dressing-room character, voted the PFA's Player of the Year in 1985, when he finally gained full international recognition. A superb signing by Kendall.

Andy Gray

Position: Centre-forward.
Joined Everton: November, 1983, £200,000 from Wolves.
Analysis: Totally transformed a team struggling near the foot of the First Division table. Once the most expensive player in Britain, most clubs believed Gray's astonishing bravery had made him injury-prone. Kendall knew better, and within months of his arrival Everton had won the F.A. Cup to end a 14-year-run without a major honour. The darling of the Goodison Park fans, Gray terrorised the Continental defences during the Cup-Winners' Cup run in 1985. Returned to Aston Villa for £150,000 following an incredible 18-month love affair with Everton.

Kevin Sheedy

Position: Left midfield.
Joined Everton: August, 1982, £100,000 from Liverpool.
Analysis: Liverpool had signed Sheedy from Hereford and were grooming him for glory, but his patience ran out after years in their reserve team and moved across Stanley Park in 1982 for First Division football. Tremendous passing ability and deadly around the box with his free-kick expertise, Sheedy's contribution of 17 goals to the 1984-85 season included a number of crucial efforts.

Gary Lineker

Position: Centre-forward.
Joined Everton: June 1985, £800,000 from Leicester.
Analysis: Kendall was none to pleased when a transfer tribunal ruled he had to pay £800,000 for the England striker from Leicester. But within months it was clear that even at that price Everton had got themselves a bargain. Everton fans, unhappy with the sale of Gray, took time to accept Lineker, but 30 goals in his first seven months more than won them over. A lethal partnership with Graeme Sharp. PFA Player of the Year and Footballer of the Year in 1985-86.

Paul Bracewell.

THE KENDALL MEN

Players signed May 1981-March 1986

Signed	Player	From	Fee	Hit or Miss
July 81	Alan Biley	Derby	£350,000	Miss
July 81	Neville Southall	Bury	£150,000	Hit
Aug 81	Mickey Thomas	Man. Utd.	£450,000	Miss
Aug 81	Alan Ainscow	Birmingham	£250,000	Miss
Aug 81	Jim Arnold	Blackburn	£175,000	Hit
Aug 81	Mick Ferguson	Coventry	£280,000	Miss
Aug 81	Mike Walsh	Bolton	£60,000	Miss
Jan 82	Adrian Heath	Stoke	£700,000	Hit
June 82	Derek Mountfield	Tranmere	£30,000	Hit
July 82	Andy King	WBA	£50,000	Miss
Aug 82	David Johnson	Liverpool	£100,000	Miss
Aug 82	Kevin Sheedy	Liverpool	£100,000	Hit
Dec 82	Peter Reid	Bolton	£60,000	Hit
June 83	Alan Harper	Liverpool	£50,000	Hit
July 83	Trevor Steven	Burnley	£300,000	Hit
Sept 83	Terry Curran	Sheff. Utd.	£150,000	Miss
Nov 83	Andy Gray	Wolves	£200,000	Hit
May 84	Paul Bracewell	Sunderland	£250,000	Hit
Sept 84	Pat Van den Hauwe	Birmingham	£100,000	Hit
Nov 84	Ian Atkins	Sunderland	£70,000	Hit
Mar 85	Paul Wilkinson	Grimsby	£250,000	?
May 85	Bobby Mimms	Rotherham	£150,000	Hit
June 85	Gary Lineker	Leicester	£800,000	Hit
Nov 85	Neil Pointon	Scunthorpe	£50,000	Hit
Dec 85	Darrin Coyle	Linfield	£40,000	?
Jan 86	Warren Aspinall	Wigan	£100,000	?

SHARP SHOOTING BLADES

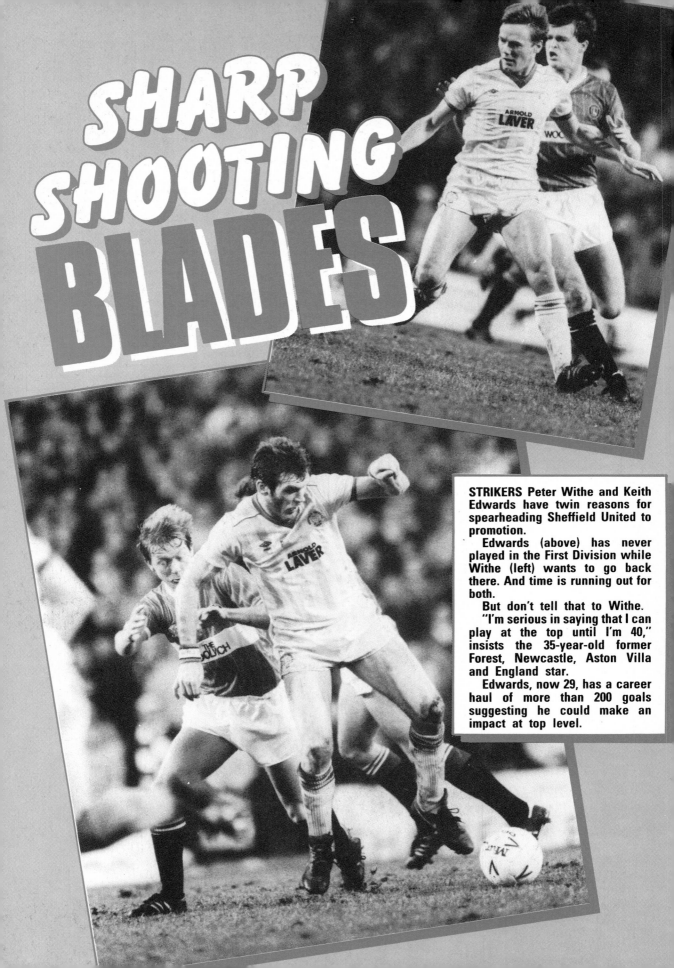

STRIKERS Peter Withe and Keith Edwards have twin reasons for spearheading Sheffield United to promotion.

Edwards (above) has never played in the First Division while Withe (left) wants to go back there. And time is running out for both.

But don't tell that to Withe.

"I'm serious in saying that I can play at the top until I'm 40," insists the 35-year-old former Forest, Newcastle, Aston Villa and England star.

Edwards, now 29, has a career haul of more than 200 goals suggesting he could make an impact at top level.

Young goalies are getting all the help they need from a Division One star

Chris Woods with young keepers at the PGL Goalkeeper School

FINDERS, KEEPERS!

England has traditionally been the home of top goalkeepers. Just lately it seems that the technique and ability of our young keeper is being overtaken by other countries. This is because goalkeeper coaching as opposed to practise is difficult to find for the enthusiastic kid.

For this reason PGL Soccer set up in 1980 the nations first goalkeeper school. Having set up the nations first soccer schools in the 70's and being part of the PGL group of companies (in 1986 over 50,000 youngsters enjoyed a PGL holiday) PGL was well placed to meet this need.

PGL director Kit Carson said "The results have been staggering. More than 3000 young keepers from every corner of the U.K. have been on our school." Letters received from young keepers and their parents show how much the courses are appreciated and for a few the coaching and PGL follow up has resulted in some 30 young keepers already signing with league clubs. "In a few years time the league clubs will have PGL keepers in their first teams who owe everything to the PGL Goalkeeper School."

Top keepers such as Bruce Grobbelaar, Ray Clemence, Paul Cooper, Paul Barron, Phil Parkes and Dai Davies have lent a hand over the years and the England international keeper Chris Woods is the goalkeeper consultant to PGL and coaches on all the current PGL Goalkeeper Schools. "What amazes me" said Chris "is the fact that most young keepers have never been coached at all in the art of goalkeeping. They really are hungry for knowledge and come back year after year."

Chris Woods' ambition is to be the England number 1. But he and Kit Carson are hoping for the day when his rival for the England spot is a young PGL keeper from the goalkeeper school.

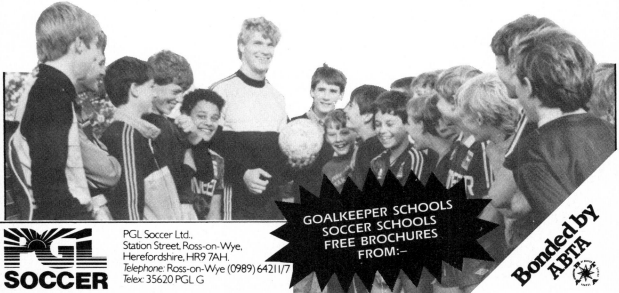

We are the Champions

LIVERPOOL completed a fantastic 1985-86 season by becoming the first club in 15 years to achieve the League and F.A. Cup double. Here skipper Alan Hansen displays the F.A. Cup to an emotional Wembley crowd after their 3-1 victory over Merseyside rivals Everton.

LIVERPOOL'S

Ian Rush scores Liverpool's third and killer goal at Wembley.

Player-manager Kenny Dalglish receives the Championship trophy at Anfield.

DOUBLE KOP

King Kenny scores the goal that won the title – against Chelsea at Stamford Bridge on the last day of the season.

WHIZZ -KIDS

Left: Clive Allen, a "millionaire" before he was 20. Right: Norman Whiteside became Britain's youngest international when he made his Northern Ireland debut in Yugoslavia.

Although there have always been players who shot to the top when still in their teens, there is no doubt that footballers mature at a much earlier age nowadays than they did 30, 40 or more years ago.

Arguably the most successful young player of the past couple of decades is Trevor Francis.

He made his debut for Birmingham City in September, 1970 at the age of 16 years 178 days and had the distinction of scoring four goals in a Second Division game two months before his 17th birthday.

Trevor became Britain's first £1million footballer at the age of 25.

An even younger player to attract big money is Spurs striker Clive Allen. He is the youngest British player ever transferred for a seven-figure fee. That was when he first moved from QPR to Arsenal in June, 1980 for £1,200,000 at the age of 19 years one month.

When Clive became Peter Shreeve's first signing for Spurs in August, 1984 his total of transfer fees had exceeded £2½million and he was still only three months past his 23rd birthday!

It's worth remembering that this Londoner scored a hat-trick in his first full game for QPR 22 days before his 18th birthday.

Another teenager to score a hat-trick in the Football League was Justin Fashanu who made his debut with Norwich City at the age of 16 years four months and got his first League goal less than two months later.

His initial League hat-trick came in a 5-1 victory over Stoke in August, 1980.

Nightmare

About this time Norwich valued Justin at nearly £2million, but when he moved to Nottingham Forest still a month short of his 20th birthday the price was £1million, a fee which made him the second youngest teenager to be transferred in Britain for a seven-figure fee. It was unfortunate that Justin had a nightmare experience with Forest.

Next to Clive Allen and Justin Fashanu the most expensive teenagers in British football have been Andy Ritchie, Steve MacKenzie and Remi Moses, each transferred for £500,000 before they were 20-years-of-age.

Brighton paid Manchester United that amount for Andy Ritchie's services in October, 1980. In August, 1981 Steve MacKenzie went from Manchester City to WBA, and a month later Albion sold Remi Moses to Manchester United.

None of these three players came to the fore at a younger age than Romford-born midfielder Steve MacKenzie. In July, 1979, when he was only 17 and had still to make his League debut, Manchester City manager Malcolm Allison thought highly enough of his prospects to pay £250,000 for Steve's transfer.

An even younger player to attract a £250,000 fee was Oldham Athletic's striker Wayne Harrison. However, Wayne had made four appearances in the Football League when Liverpool clinched this player's transfer with Wayne less than two months past his 17th birthday. That was in January, 1985 when Liverpool loaned Wayne back to Oldham for a further two months.

In the 80's no player has matured more rapidly than Manchester United's powerful young Irishman Norman Whiteside. After making his League debut before his 17th birthday and scoring his first League goal eight days later he became Britain's youngest international when called upon by N. Ireland to play in Yugoslavia at the age of 17 years 42 days, only four months older than the great Pelé was when the Brazilian made his international debut.

Talking of internationals Luther Blissett was the youngest player to score a hat-trick in his first full England game (v Luxembourg at Wembley in

players destined to become teenage soccer stars

December, 1982) since Everton's Fred Pickering did so against the USA in May, 1964. Luther was aged 24 years nine months.

Making your international debut is certainly a nerve racking experience, but what more testing senior debut for any Scottish youngster than playing in a Rangers-Celtic derby? Rangers' John MacDonald not only made his debut in this particular fixture but also scored a goal in a 2-2 draw — age 18 years four months.

Deadly Derek

Another Rangers teenager to make his debut in this clash of the Auld Enemies was Derek Johnstone. He earned a place in the record books because he was still 11 days short of his 17th birthday when he made his debut for Rangers in the Scottish League Cup Final of 1970 and scored the winning goal against Celtic!

Other teenagers who scored when making their senior League debuts in recent years include Jason Dozzell for Ipswich Town v Coventry City, in February, 1984 (age 16 years 57 days), Terry Connor for Leeds United v WBA,

in November, 1979 (eight days short of his 17th birthday), Paul McStay, Celtic v Aberdeen at Pittodrie, in January, 1982 (17 years three months), and Andy Gray, Dundee United v Dumbarton, in August, 1973 (17 years nine months).

At 21 years six months Andy Gray became the youngest player to top the First Division scoring list since Jimmy Greaves.

This was with Aston Villa in 1976-77 when he actually tied for top place with Arsenal's Malcolm MacDonald, each with 25 goals.

We have, of course, just mentioned the greatest teenage goalscoring star of all time in Jimmy Greaves, a player who topped the First Division scoring

list for the first time with Chelsea in 1958-59, getting most of his total of 32 League goals before his 19th birthday in February of that campaign.

Jimmy, who later went on to become a striking sensation with Tottenham and England, first scored as many as four goals in a First Division game (against Portsmouth at Stamford Bridge in a 7-4 Chelsea victory, Christmas Day 1977) at the age of 17 years 10 months.

However, comparisons between Jimmy Greaves and more recent young scoring stars would be unfair for Jimmy Greaves' talent was unique.

But what a fantastic target for any ambitious youngster with fame and fortune on his mind to set his sights on!

Trevor Francis was just 16 when he shot four goals for Birmingham in a Second Division game.

HARD-WORKING

The men who get the goals carry the heaviest burden in football. Here four of the best face a grilling on the game's most difficult job...

	JOHN DEEHAN Norwich	GARY LINEKER Everton
When did you decide to become a striker?	In my first game as a schoolboy I positioned myself up-front. Seeing Geoff Hurst score a hat-trick in England's 1966 World Cup win — I was nine at the time — made me want to be like him.	Ever since I can remember I've wanted to be a goalscorer. I was particularly encouraged by a schoolmaster, George Sims, and I'll always be grateful to him.
Do you still recall a great goal from early in your career?	I was going through a lean period with Aston Villa. We were playing Birmingham City and there was 15 minutes to go. I let fly from the edge of their box — and the ball shot into the top corner for the winner.	It may surprise you to know that I've never yet scored what I consider to be a *great* goal. That is, one that's hammered from outside the box into a top corner. All my goals so far have come from close range.
A recent one?	Norwich were playing Watford away and the boss expected a non-stop bombardment so he asked me to drop back to centre-half. I took Watford by surprise by pressing forward from the half-way line and driving a 30-yarder into their net. We drew 2-2.	As I've said I don't get great goals. But I was well pleased with the hat-trick I scored against Man. City last season.
What type of goal do you regard as your trademark?	Arriving at the near-post and either scoring from a glancing header or the side of a foot.	Before I came to Everton, it was running on to a through ball and slotting it home. Since I've been at Goodison I score more with my head.
Worst injury?	An ankle injury that once kept me sidelined for three months. Agony in every respect.	A groin strain from playing in a testimonial for Keith Burkinshaw forced me to drop out of England's South American tour in 1984.
Which 'keeper do you regard as the hardest to beat?	There are no easy 'keepers around. And for me the hardest to face is young Peter Fox of Stoke City. I've never beaten him! Mind you, I'm grateful I don't have to try to get the ball past our Chris Woods.	It's got to be Peter Shilton, run close by Norwich City's Chris Woods, whose marvellous 'keeping restricted me to only one goal in a Super Cup tie last season.
Do you have special training?	We do a lot of close-in work at Norwich. Headers and side-foots from six to eight yards so that when a chance arises in a match we will react instinctively and not panic.	The emphasis at Everton is on perfecting strikers' finishing, probably the same at every other club. Keeping things simple is the watchword.
A lucky/unlucky ground?	I enjoy Upton Park where I've scored quite a few goals and rarely come off losing. Goodison Park is something of a jinx ground as I tend to waste chances there.	Anfield, home of Liverpool, a notorious graveyard for strikers. I opened the scoring there for Leicester in a 2-0 League win in December, 1984. Villa Park, though, has been unlucky for me, particularly when Leicester lost there in an F.A. Cup Semi.

STRIKERS

John Deehan.

Gary Lineker scores again.

Mick Harford.

Kerry Dixon.

MICK HARFORD Luton	KERRY DIXON Chelsea
I began my career with Lincoln City in midfield. When a striker got injured I took his place up front — and I've been there ever since!	My dad played as a striker for Coventry and Luton and later in non-League football where I watched him as a lad. Although he's taught me a lot, our styles are very different.
Could I ever forget the goal that kept Birmingham City in the First Division? The match was a last-gasp affair, against Coventry City away, and I scored in our one-nil win.	I have mixed feelings about the goal I hit for Reading at Doncaster. I cut in from the left and drove the ball home with my right foot. It was one of four we scored. Trouble was, Doncaster got five!
It was a 30-yarder against Leicester City on New Year's Day, 1986, the first of a fantastic hat-trick. What a way to start the year!	A cracking, perfectly-timed volley from a back-header by Pat Nevin in our 2-0 win over Ipswich at Portman Road last season.
The header at the far post. My trademark was featured in that hat-trick!	There isn't a typical Dixon goal in my opinion. My goals come in a variety of ways, but I feel I need to widen my range.
A hernia injury sustained with Birmingham put me out of the game for three long, long months.	A severe pelvic injury put me out of action for two months at Reading.
The pair up on Merseyside — Bruce Grobbelaar and Neville Southall — can be soul-destroying. But Watford's Tony Coton — my friend from Birmingham City days together — runs them close.	Peter Shilton is the master. If there's a finer number one in the World I haven't heard about him.
Yes — in the penalty box, where we practice shooting, turning, and selling "dummies".	All aspects of a striker's role are worked on, with no accent on any particular skill.
I've always done well at St. James' Park, where I was once a player. The electric atmosphere there gives me a real lift. I never feel the same at Goodison Park!	No ground stands out as being either lucky or unlucky for me. The breaks — good and bad — seem to even themselves out wherever I play.

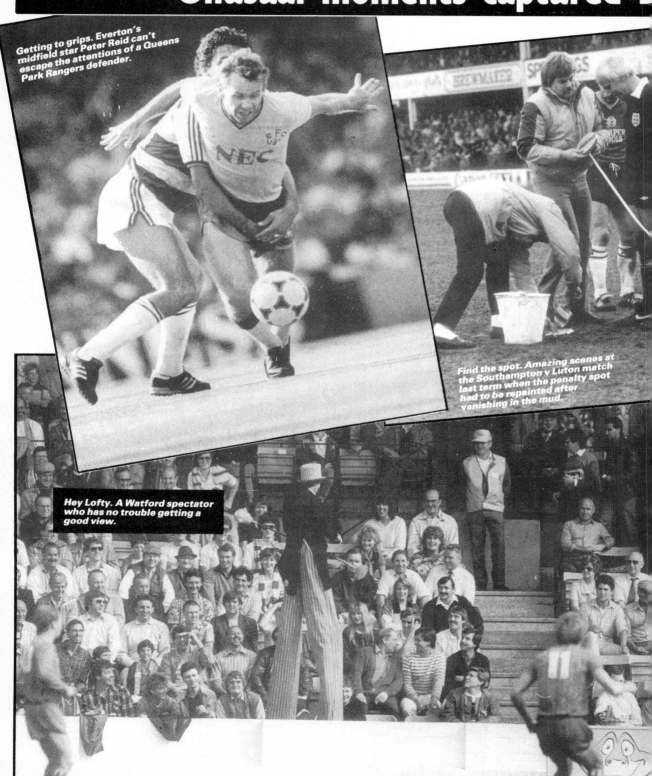

Getting to grips. Everton's midfield star Peter Reid can't escape the attentions of a Queens Park Rangers defender.

Find the spot. Amazing scenes at the Southampton v Luton match last term when the penalty spot had to be repainted after vanishing in the mud.

Hey Lofty. A Watford spectator who has no trouble getting a good view.

CAMERA

High diving. Tottenham's Gary Mabbutt goes overboard during his club's 0-0 draw with Arsenal at Highbury last season.

A demolition job. An appropriate notice as Oxford fans celebrate their team's 4–1 victory at Chelsea last season.

1

OXFORD United, who only 25 years ago were playing non-League football, made their first appearance at Wembley on April 20th, 1986 and convincingly beat favourites Queens Park Rangers to win the Milk Cup Final.

Oxford took the lead in the 40th minute with a goal from Man of the Match Trevor Hebberd.

OXFORD'S H

3

Jeremy Charles makes victory a formality by scoring Oxford's late third goal.

Ray Houghton blasts the ball past Rangers 'keeper Paul Barron to put Oxford two up.

BOMBERS

We are the Champions

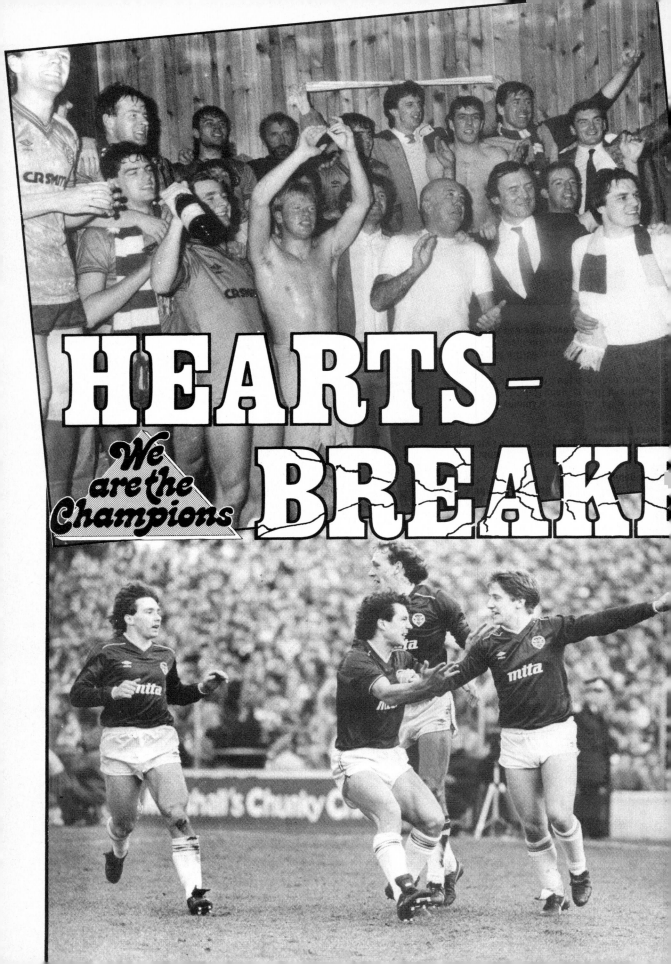

HEARTS-
BREAKE

We are the Champions

RS

Above left: Celtic sensationally pipped Hearts to the 1985-86 Premier Division title with a 5-0 win at St. Mirren in their last game of the season.

Left: Hearts enjoyed an amazing unbeaten run of 31 games, including this 3-1 victory over Rangers.

Above right: Aberdeen's Tommy McQueen (right) and Hearts' John Robertson battle for possession in the Scottish Cup Final.

Right: Aberdeen skipper Willie Miller with the Scottish Cup after their 3-0 Hampden triumph over luckless Hearts.

Dynamo Kiev won the 1985-86 Cup-Winners' Cup Final with a fine 3-0 victory over Atletico Madrid. Here Kiev's famous striker Blokhin is challenged by Madrid defender Ruiz.

EURO

Barcelona boss Terry Venables reflects on the utter despair of losing the European Cup Final to Steaua Bucharest in Seville.

Bucharest's Jordanescu (left) and 'keeper Ducadam with the European Cup after their shock penalty shoot-out victory.

Specials

Real Madrid (white shirts) lifted Spanish hearts by capturing the UEFA Cup last season, beating IFC Cologne 5-3 on aggregate.

LAUGH LINES

"Dedicated our lot. They train to the last minute."

"I saw it on telly, son — a forty yard header — I'm proud of you."

"Let's get there early, you said — and find a good spot."

GRAEME SOUNESS
Scotland

The day Coventry City allowed their dark haired young centre-forward, Mark Hateley, to leave the First Division and seek a new career with Portsmouth, they wrote a new chapter in the history of England's international progress. The big, lean and lethal striker made a instant impact in Division Two and following a successful summer tour with England in South America was finally snapped up by Italian giants AC Milan in the summer of 1984 Milan forked out £1 million, Hateley, son of a famous striking father Tony, scored priceless goals — and enhanced his new international reputation with similar form for Bobby Robson. People recall the latter stages of England's World Cup Qualifying Group Three triumph when they struggled to find the devastating form demanded by the Wembley fans, but tend to forget the crucial goals he scored earlier — and the way he bravely shook off a nasty knee injury to sustain his vast popularity among the fanatical fans in Italy.

HANDY ANDY

*J*ust when they needed it most Aston Villa's fans received a great shot in the arm when Andy Gray was re-signed, from Everton. Gray, the brave, bold and always battling centre-forward they sold to Wolves had done his bit for the Molineux club, moved on to help Everton to become Champions of England, FA Cup Winners and Cup Winner's Cup holders. And despite injuries — the Scot's style of play always put his health at risk — Gray rekindled his international career and helped Scotland reach the 1986 World Cup Finals. Now Andy is scoring goals for Aston Villa the club he always said he loved.

GRID RIDDLE

Answers on page 125

Identify the mystery men

BIRTH	Dorchester 1st August, 1963	Berwick 21st September, 1963	Liverpool 20th November, 1961	Hillingdon 14th September, 1956
POSITION	Defender	Midfield	Defender	Midfield
FIRST CLUB	Oxford Utd	Burnley	Liverpool	Chelsea
BIG BREAK	Southampton March, 1982	£325,000 Everton signing, 1983	Norwich November, 1980	Manchester Utd, August 1979
STATUS	England debut v Wales, May 1984	England debut v N. Ireland, Feb '85	England debut v Brazil, June 1984	England debut v Italy, May '76

Allen mark three

Martin Allen has finally stepped from the shadows of his better known cousins, Clive and Paul, and is now ready and able to meet Tottenham's big money stars on equal terms.

Martin, at 21 the baby of the trio, has worked hard to achieve the big breakthrough.

Rangers boss, Jim Smith, called Martin into the team early last season. He took the chance eagerly to earn rave reviews.

But it was not easy for him in the early days, with all the headlines going to the other members of the family.

"When I was trying to make my way as a young apprentice at Rangers, Clive and Paul were already big news. People were making comparisons — and although it was not really fair I accepted it as inevitable," says Martin.

"Clive had been involved in a £1m transfer to Arsenal and Paul made history as the youngest player ever to appear in an F.A. Cup Final — with West Ham against Arsenal. Then he made headlines with that move to Spurs in the summer of 1985.

"So people were naturally looking to see what the third member of the family was capable of. Hopefully I have been able to show them.

Wembley dream

"I would really love to play against the other two in a Cup Final at Wembley.

"That would be a real highlight — a special occasion to stretch family loyalties!"

The brothers that produced this trio of talented young players all have footballing backgrounds.

Clive's father, Les, was in the Tottenham team that did the double in 1961 and also played for Chelsea and QPR — where he had a spell as manager.

Dennis Allen, father of Martin, played for Charlton and Reading and is now general manager at Exeter.

Paul's Dad, Ron, seemed set for a promising career — until it was ended by injury at a young age.

"The pressures I faced early on, trying to match the exploits of the other two, have now gone," claims Martin.

"I shall concentrate only on staying in the Rangers side and playing well. If I do that I know there's every chance of making a name for myself."

Smith describes Allen Mark 3 as a youngster always willing to listen and with a tremendous desire to do well. "His attitude has impressed me a lot," he says.

Martin Allen (above) aims to prove himself as good a player as cousin Clive (right).

TOP MARKS FOR BRENNAN

As the top stars streamed away from Portman Road in the wake of Bobby Robson's appointment as England manager, Ipswich had to unearth a whole new crop of youngsters. One undoubted success is Mark Brennan (below, in action against Tottenham's Tony Galvin). Apprentice Brennan became a First Division player aged 18 and while no great shakes in the scoring stakes, displayed maturity and composure on the ball, delivering killer passes for Kevin Wilson, Mich D. 'Avray and Jason Dozzell — another precocious product — as Town battled for First Division survival. Mark Brennan is a name to watch!

Battler Beardsley

Peter Beardley's switchback career finally settled in the North East where he established himself as one of Newcastle United's most exciting forwards. But the Geordie-born striker had to see a good chunk of the football world before coming 'home'. More than 100 League games for Carlisle club were followed by two spells with Canadian club Vancouver Whitecaps, either side of a brief time with Manchester United. But when The Magpies came in for him Beardsley saw off departing stars such as Kevin Keegan and Chris Waddle to become the idol of Tyneside.

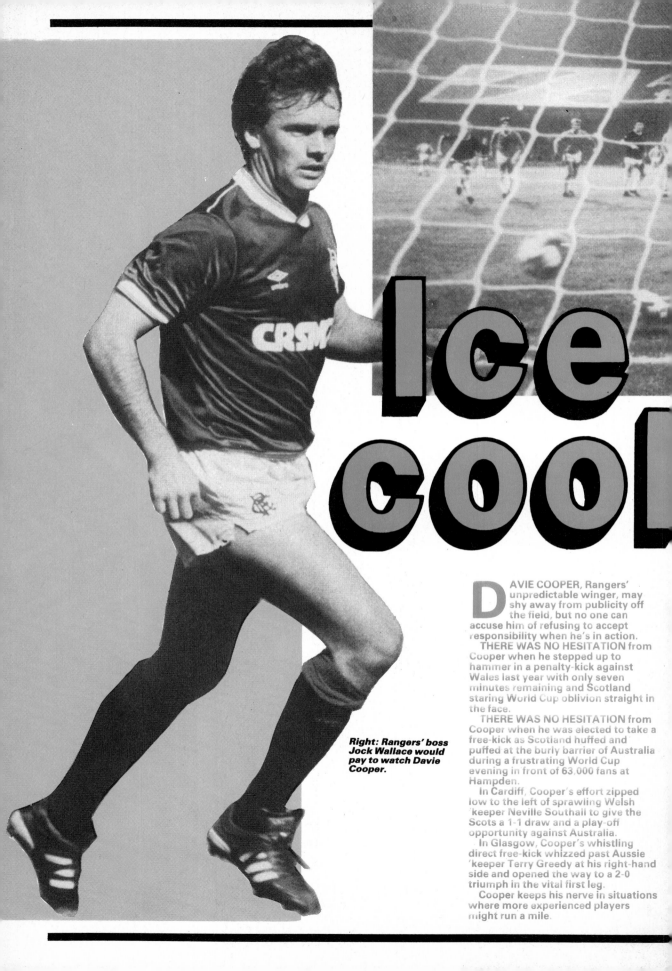

Ice cool

Right: Rangers' boss Jock Wallace would pay to watch Davie Cooper.

DAVIE COOPER, Rangers' unpredictable winger, may shy away from publicity off the field, but no one can accuse him of refusing to accept responsibility when he's in action.

THERE WAS NO HESITATION from Cooper when he stepped up to hammer in a penalty-kick against Wales last year with only seven minutes remaining and Scotland staring World Cup oblivion straight in the face.

THERE WAS NO HESITATION from Cooper when he was elected to take a free-kick as Scotland huffed and puffed at the burly barrier of Australia during a frustrating World Cup evening in front of 63,000 fans at Hampden.

In Cardiff, Cooper's effort zipped low to the left of sprawling Welsh 'keeper Neville Southall to give the Scots a 1-1 draw and a play-off opportunity against Australia.

In Glasgow, Cooper's whistling direct free-kick whizzed past Aussie 'keeper Terry Greedy at his right-hand side and opened the way to a 2-0 triumph in the vital first leg.

Cooper keeps his nerve in situations where more experienced players might run a mile.

Above: Cooper scores from the penalty-spot v Wales to keep Scotland in the World Cup.
Right: Davie takes on the Aussies in typical style.

Cooper

His Ibrox manager Jock Wallace says: "The boy simply oozes class and, as he has proved to everyone, he has a big match temperament.

"He's the type of player I would pay to watch. He's a crowd pleaser, a real natural.

"You can't tell him how to play. He does so much by instinct. He's deadly with free-kicks and penalties. He hits the ball like a Brazilian.

"He can make it dip and swerve and he's left a lot of goalkeepers utterly helpless with his accuracy from a variety of ranges.

"I used to be a goalkeeper and I wouldn't fancy facing up to one of Coop's efforts. You never know how he's going to bend them."

Cooper — known as 'Moody Blue' — is an enigmatic figure and rarely gives interviews. He won't talk on the radio because he doesn't like the sound of his own voice.

And on the night he was the Guest of Honour of the official Rangers Supporters' Association to pick up their Player of the Year award he was nowhere to be seen.

He doesn't like making public speeches!

But the wing wonder has that uncanny knack of making the ball sit up and talk — and he does it with amazing regularity.

When he was asked about how he felt taking that lifeline penalty-kick against the Welsh with only seven minutes remaining, Cooper replied: "I knew I would have to hit it well to beat such a good goalkeeper as Neville Southall.

"I made up my mind to keep it low and aim for a corner. Thankfully, it went in. The importance of such a goal didn't dawn on me until after the match."

Cooper, of course, doesn't just turn it on while appearing on the international platform.

Rangers fans glory in the memory of his superb efforts and Hibs 'keeper Alan Rough, who guarded the Scots goal during the second-half of that tense Cardiff encounter, is still trying to fathom how Cooper beat him with a 30-yard free-kick during the sides' meeting in the League Cup semi-final at Ibrox earlier in the season.

"Only Davie can hit them like that," says Rough ruefully. "When he connects you're lucky to see the ball never mind save it."

Yes, Davie Cooper might not talk a lot, but he has had a big say in the fortunes of Scotland and Rangers.

Barnes stormer

I t took John Barnes a long time to live down that famous solo goal with which he devastated Brazil in Rio back in June, 1984.

It sparked a 2-0 win for England, sealed by a superb header from Mark Hateley. The world talked of both young players long and loud. But while Hateley became a cult figure with AC Milan and scored vital goals in England qualification for Mexico, Barnes was forever being criticised for not producing similar moments of inspiration when playing for his country.

What the critics failed to appreciate is that such a goal comes, perhaps, once in a lifetime. Barnes had many sound and hard working games for Bobby Robson afterwards, but time and again he read hurtful words about his contribution. Fortunately, in Graham Taylor, he has a manager who knows how to lift his men. Taylor said: "John is the best orthodox winger in the game at the moment. No question." Who is arguing now?

When Everton signed Trevor Steven from Burnley they had to wait a while for the youngster to reproduce his form at Turf Moor. But when Howard Kendall did get Steven going — he went all the way to England's World Cup campaign.

Rejected by Doncaster and Now it's
FULL SPEEDIE

David and his sidekick Kerry Dixon are one of the deadliest double acts in the country.

Ever since teaming up at Stamford Bridge they have terrorised defenders and goalkeepers in a blaze of goals.

But it hasn't always been plain sailing. David admits: "Right at the start of our partnership I used to give Kerry some terrible stick.

"I felt he was shooting from false positions. He'd have been much better playing me in with a pass. We'd have got even more goals that way.

"It wasn't long, however, before we overcame the problems. We had to work hard at developing an understanding; it didn't just happen overnight.

"Now we know each other inside out. I think the fact that Kerry is such a big lad, while I'm smaller, makes us ideal partners.

"Little and Large if you like!"

When David was rejected by Doncaster Rovers he found himself in good company.

Because years earlier they had also shown the door to Kevin Keegan — he went on to captain England.

"I had trials at Everton as well as Doncaster," he recalls, "and the answer was the same on both occasions.

"They thought I was too small and that put them off. But, if anything, being turned down made me all the more determined to make the grade. I wanted to prove them wrong."

Eventually his luck changed and after a spell as a part-timer he was given a two-year contract by Barnsley, at that time managed by Jim Iley.

He was a midfield player in those days and it wasn't until his second season with Darlington that he was switched to the firing line.

"I won the Player of the Year award at Darlington in my first season when I was playing in midfield," David remembers, "and I volunteered to give it a go up front when the regular strikers were injured.

"Everything clicked straightaway. I got 18 goals that year and I'm pleased to say I've been banging them in regularly ever since."

Don't let his Yorkshire accent fool you. David Speedie is Scottish through and through.

His fifth birthday was still some way off when his parents 'emigrated' South of the border from Fife where he was born.

The closure of the local coal mine put his father, Robert, out of work and rather than face up to life on the dole he decided on a move to England.

"But all the years I was growing up I never felt anything but Scottish," says David. "Dad was Rangers-daft and it was always my dream to play for Scotland."

That dream came true when David lined up against England at Hampden in May, 1985, and helped the Scots to a memorable 1-0 victory.

And the Hampden crowd was swelled by the presence of several members of the Speedie clan. "Most of my relatives are North of the border,"

Everton.
AHEAD

future."

Don't expect David Speedie to change his ways just because suspension has forced him on to the sidelines more than once.

"If I changed I'd be a different player. I don't think I'd be half as effective. And that could mean the end of my days with Chelsea and Scotland," he points out.

"I'm not proud of my disciplinary record and I'm not exactly innocent.

David made his Scotland debut against England at Hampden in May, 1985.

says David, "and it costs me a small fortune to buy tickets for them all!"

Former Chelsea chief John Neal is the man who put David on the road to stardom.

"I'll always be indebted to John," says the Stamford Bridge star. "He took me under his wing and made me a First Division player.

"When Chelsea picked me up from Darlington I thought I was a half decent player, nothing more. I was ambitious, of course, but without John Neal I doubt if I'd have gone as far in the game.

"We struggled a bit in my first season at Chelsea, mind you, and it was touch and go for a while whether we'd stay in the Second Division.

"But the following season there was a bit of a clear-out, Kerry Dixon arrived and we won the Second Division title.

"It was sad when John Neal stepped down but both the new manager, John Hollins, and his assistant, Ian McNeill, have a tremendous influence on my career and I really believe Chelsea can go from strength to strength in the

Some of the criticism that comes my way is deserved. I'll admit that.

"But a lot of it is over-exaggerated. I would never dream of committing a tackle that might put an opponent out of the game. I'm not malicious."

The 26-year-old goal ace would like nothing more than to discard the bad-boy image.

"People say I get involved in incidents that don't concern me but I won't just stand back and see team-mates clobbered. Of course it concerns me and I'm entitled to draw the referee's attention to it.

"But the people who label me a troublemaker have got it all wrong. From what I read in some papers I'm virtually a thug and that's rubbish.

"I'm enthusiastic, I hate to lose and maybe I get carried away now and again. But that's the way I am — and I'm not going to change!"

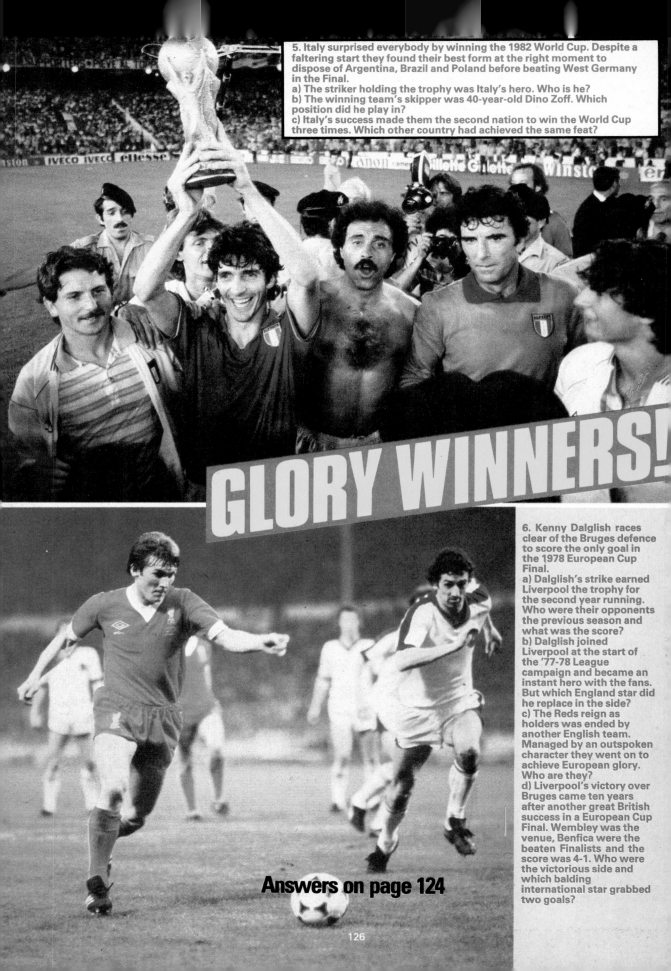

5. Italy surprised everybody by winning the 1982 World Cup. Despite a faltering start they found their best form at the right moment to dispose of Argentina, Brazil and Poland before beating West Germany in the Final.
a) The striker holding the trophy was Italy's hero. Who is he?
b) The winning team's skipper was 40-year-old Dino Zoff. Which position did he play in?
c) Italy's success made them the second nation to win the World Cup three times. Which other country had achieved the same feat?

GLORY WINNERS!

6. Kenny Dalglish races clear of the Bruges defence to score the only goal in the 1978 European Cup Final.
a) Dalglish's strike earned Liverpool the trophy for the second year running. Who were their opponents the previous season and what was the score?
b) Dalglish joined Liverpool at the start of the '77-78 League campaign and became an instant hero with the fans. But which England star did he replace in the side?
c) The Reds reign as holders was ended by another English team. Managed by an outspoken character they went on to achieve European glory. Who are they?
d) Liverpool's victory over Bruges came ten years after another great British success in a European Cup Final. Wembley was the venue, Benfica were the beaten Finalists and the score was 4-1. Who were the victorious side and which balding international star grabbed two goals?

Answers on page 124

126